WAKING UP
FROM OUR NIGHTMARE

THE 9/11/01 CRIMES
IN NEW YORK CITY

I/R
2004

Irresistible/Revolutionary (I/R)
POB 33-0178, San Francisco, CA 94133-2909

Includes bibliographical references

1. September 11, 2001 Attacks in the United States
2. Physical Evidence in the Collapses of World Trade Center Buildings 1, 2, and 7
3. Explanations for the Collapses of World Trade Center Buildings 1, 2, and 7
4. Ownership of World Trade Center Buildings 1, 2, and 7
5. Trauma through Media
6. Pretexts for War
7. Financiers of the 'New World Order' (Rothschilds, Rockefellers, ...).
8. Federal Reserve System and Federal Reserve Bank of New York
9. Council on Foreign Relations
10. Illegal Narcotics' Revenues
11. Alternatives to Debt-Based Banking
12. Alternatives to Fossil-Fuel Energy
13. Community-Based Solutions

Additional copies of this book may be ordered from I/R at the POB above or from wtc7.net and www.wireonfire.com/donpaul/ . $10 each for 1 to 4 copies, $9 each for 5 to 9 copies, and $8 each for 10 or more copies. Special price of $6 for 25 or more copies. Price includes shipping within the U. S.

An electronic companion to this book, with hyperlinked URLs, can be found at http://wtc7.net/books/wakingup/

First edition
ISBN 0-94309605-12

Thanks again to Chris Carlisle. Thanks also to Gregg Roberts.

Front cover photograph by Gulnara Samoilova/AP.
See more of her work at www.gulnarasamoilova.com .

The only visual proof that mass-media has offered of Osama bin Laden's guilt for the 9/11/01 crimes is a video released by the U.S. Government on 12/13/01. It's supposed to show bin Laden and associates meeting in Kandahar, Afghanistan on 11/9/01. The stout 'mastermind' of 11/9/01 differs markedly from prior records of Osama bin Laden: his nose is shorter, his cheekbones lower, and his forehead narrower. Compare the Osama in the November 2001 video presented by CNN and NPR with the Osama of 1998 and September 2001. [1]

Osama the Gaunt
in December 1998
as presented by
mass-media

Osama the Stout
in November 2001
as presented by
mass-media

Fictions about the guilt of Osama bin Laden and al Qaeda for " '9/11' " persist.

At the dinner shown shown on the [November 2001] videotape, bin Laden praised the attacks on the World Trade Center ... " We calculated in advance the number of casualties from the enemy, who would be killed, based on the position of the towers. We calculated that the floors that would be hit would be three or four floors, " bin Laden said on the tape. " I was thinking that the fire from the gas in the plane would melt the iron structure of the building and collapse the area where the plane hit and all the floors above it only. This is all we had hoped for. "

Associated Press, Abdullah al-Shihri, July 14, 2004

Our enemy is twofold: al Qaeda, a stateless network of terrorists that struck us on 9/11; and a radical ideological movement in the Islamic world, inspired in part by al Qaeda, which has spawned terrorist groups and violence around the globe.

The 9/11 Commission Report from The National Commission on Terrorist Attacks, page 363, July 22, 2004

A NOTE ABOUT THIS BOOK'S PUNCTUATION

In regard to quotation from sources, we follow British convention as to the placement of quotation marks in relation to periods or commas. We also follow British convention in the indication of written quotes by single quotation marks and of spoken quotes by double quotation marks.

More originally, we enclose in single quotation marks nested inside double quotation marks any phrase whose credibility or psychological effect we believe is deserving of more examination than that given in shorthand definitions by Governments and mass-media—e.g., " '9/11' ", " 'Attack on America' ", and so forth. (Conversely, double quotation marks nested inside of single quotation marks indicate that a publication is quoting someone's verbal expression—i.e., the *SFGate.com*'s quote of Dick Cheney on page 54.)

We've adopted this original quote-within-a-quote signification in order to counter a kind of echo-effect that occurs from definitions by government officials that are then quoted by corporate media and then repeated by the public at large.

One premise of this book is that the major crimes of 9/11/01 were an acutely calculated assault on people's psyches. Part of this assault involved repetition of primal images and phrases that were themselves used by government and media to define and blunt stupendously complex and criminal events—e.g., 'TERROR', 'US ATTACKED', 'EVIL ACTS', etc. Thus we all were blinded, much like deer by headlights.

Our nested quotes are an effort to disempower such blinding definitions—to take away the corporate government's echo-effect—and instead to empower thoughtful examination.

Contents

WTC 7

The Twin Towers

The Financiers Behind " '9/11' "

Cooperative Solutions

Endnotes

Introduction

Man-made trauma, however, is often more difficult to deal with [than natural disasters] because frequently the perpetrators still live in close proximity to victims—thereby providing constant reminders of the past, as well as the threat of further incidents.

Eric Brahm, 'Trauma Healing', 2003 [1]

On September 11, 2001 the people of the world and especially the United States received serial traumas over a time period about as long as that of feature-length movie.

At 8:46 Eastern Daylight Time one Boeing 767 airliner flew into the North Tower of the World Trade Center in New York City. 17 minutes later another Boeing 767 airliner tore into the World Trade Center's South Tower, exploding into a spectacular fireball. 40 minutes later, TV networks showed the devastated portion of the Pentagon's west wedge that was supposedly hit by a 757 airliner. Less than 20 minutes after this assault on the symbol of U.S. military might, the 110-story South Tower of the World Trade Center collapsed, blowing more than 100,000 tons of powdered concrete and shards of steel and aluminum over lower Manhattan. And at 10:28—less than a half hour after the South Tower's explosive fall and one hour fourty-two minutes after the crash into WTC 1—the North Tower also collapsed into a mushrooming cloud of rubble, leaving a smoldering ruin.

As networks repeated footage of the Towers' collapse, we viewers absorbed the horrors and imagined how many thousands of people must have died. Our jaws dropped. Our eyes blinked. Our bellies ached. We felt as if we ourselves had been hit. Unfathomable suffering passed through screens to us.

Much later in that day, at 5:20 PM EDT, another skyscraper, the 47-story World Trade Center Building 7, collapsed into its own foundation (or footprint) in less than seven seconds. WTC 7's mysterious, unexplained fall was much less widely broadcast than the Twin Towers'.

Now, three years after " '9/11' ", we hope to show in this illustrated book that both WTC 7 and the Twin Towers were demolished by internal explosives. We hope to show that the crimes committed in New York City on 9/11/01 could not have been committed by " 'al Queda' ", nor by any other group of terrorists except one with access to the internal, structural-steel columns of WTC 7 and the Twin Towers. We hope to show that the crimes in New York City on " '9/11' "—and hence all the crimes of the " 'Attack on America' "—must have been principally perpetrated within the United States Government.

On the night of 9/11/01, the *Washington Post* online published a piece by Henry Kissinger that echoed words from Zbignew Brzezinski (1997) and the 'Project for a New American Century' (2000). Kissinger's piece said at 9:04 EDT:

... the government should be charged with a systematic response that, one hopes, will end the way that the attack on Pearl Harbor ended

TERROR   ATTACKED   BASTARDS!   DEVASTATION
          ATTACKED   OUTRAGE   Thousands feared dead
TERROR   AMERICA   'Unyielding anger'   in terrorist attacks on U.S.
          ATTACKED
TERROR   America Under Attack   'FIND THE COURAGE'   How many dead?
TERROR   ATTACK ON AMERICA   WHAT NOW?   ATTACKS SHATTER NATION
          U.S. UNDER ATTACK   AMERICA SAVAGED,
TERROR   U.S. ATTACKED   AMERICA'S   FOREVER CHANGED
                          BLOODIEST DAY
TERROR   U.S. ATTACKED   NATION MOURNS
Bloody terror   ASSAULT
          U.S. attacked   ON AMERICA   'None of us will
Terror   U.S. ATTACKED   ever forget'
strike   U.S. attacked   'EVIL ACTS'   "NONE OF US WILL EVER
                                         FORGET THIS DAY"
Terrorists   Act of evil
strike U.S.   AMERICA'S   'MASS MURDER'
          DARKEST DAY   ACT
Terror strikes U.S.   Darkest hour   OF   UNTHINKABLE
TERROR HITS HOME   WAR   'OUR NATION SAW EVIL'
          DAY OF DEATH
TERROR HITS HOME   BUSH VOWS
          A NEW DAY   TO STRIKE BACK
TERROR   OF INFAMY   'ACT OF WAR'
BEYOND BELIEF   A Day Of Terror   ACT OF WAR   AMERICA VOWS REVENGE AS
Terror and disbelief   Day of terror   War at home   TERROR CLAIMS THOUSANDS
Terrorized   TERROR, NOW ANGER   FREEDOM   Bush vows terrorist
                          SPECIAL REPORT   acts to be avenged
TERROR'S TOLL   America's nightmare   UNDER SIEGE   'AMERICA'S FREEDOM
                                         WILL BE DEFENDED'

Above are banner headlines in 63 U.S. newspapers on 9/12/01. Five of these 63 newspapers' front page headlines referred to Pearl Harbor. Only one ran a photograph of the collapse of either Twin Tower on its front page.

We also hope to show why the terrible crimes of " '9/11' " were committed. The financiers who have most benefited from the invasions and wars that followed from " '9/11' " —financiers who control Corporations that traffic in oil and gas, armaments, illegal narcotics, and enormous debt—are also the financiers who fund, select, and direct office holders of the United States and other Governments. They needed a horrific event such as " '9/11' " to sustain their foundering systems and further their admitted agenda of a 'New World Order'. Opium from Afghanistan appears to be as important to their supranational economy as oil from Iraq.

We know that officials within the U.S. Government and employees of financiers wrote before 9/11/01 that a shock like 'Pearl Harbor' was needed to stir the U.S. public toward war. In his 1997 book The Grand Chessboard Zbigniew Brzezinski, National Security Adviser to Democratic President Jimmy Carter and co-founder of the supranational Trilateral Commission with banker David Rockefeller, wrote that ' a truly massive and widely perceived external threat ' would be needed to bring the U.S. into a 'supportive mood' for international war such as might lead to desired control of Central Asia and the Middle East. Brzezinski remembered 'the shock of the Japanese attack on Pearl Harbor' as providing such a threat. Three years later, in September 2000, the Republicans' 'Project for a New American Century' urged more funding for the U.S. military so that the U.S. could ' fight and decisively win multiple, simultaneous major theater wars '. PNAC wrote that such an increase needed, however, ' some catastrophic and catalyzing event—like a new Pearl Harbor '. [2]

This book will show that the same families of financiers who profited from all sides in World War II are now profiting from the " 'War on Terror' ". Some among them were or are also integral to Buildings of the World Trade Center. David Rockefeller, for one, was prime mover behind completion of the entire WTC at the same time as he chaired the Council on Foreign Relations, a private group whose directors were described in *Esquire* magazine in 1962 as 'that part of the Establishment that guides our destiny as a nation'.

We'll see, too, that the current Chairman of the CFR, Peter G. Peterson, is also Chairman of the Blackstone Group, an investment banking firm that took over the mortgage for World Trade Center Building 7 in October 2000. The Blackstone Group and two other mortage-holders for WTC 7, Banc of America Securities and General Motors Acceptance Corporation, thus shared in the insurance payment of $861 million that was awarded to them and the WTC 7's developer, Silverstein Properties, in February 2002. A total of $378 million had been invested in WTC 7 prior to this Buildings' admitted demolition (admitted by developer Larry Silverstein in a Public Broadcasting System documentary of September 2002, we'll see). WTC 7 and the Twin Towers together needed more than $1 billion in renovations to compete as desirable office-space in lower Manhattan prior to their destruction.

We'll see that from 2000 until 2004, Peter G. Peterson was also Chairman of the Federal Reserve Bank of New York, the most consequential of the Federal Reserve System's 12 regional Banks because it 'sets interest rates and controls the daily supply of and price of currency throughout the U.S.' [3] We'll see how determinative the "Fed" and its interest rates and other manipulations are to the financial stability of the U.S. public and to the living conditions of working people worldwide. We'll see, too, that the "Fed" is owned by private Banks, most of them under European control, and that the Rothschild family has profited from terror and war since the American Revolution. We'll see how drug money is laundered through Banks and how the International Monetary Fund exploits billions of people, in order to sustain precarious Western economies.

We'll see that the "Fed" and other major financial institutions that depend on the U.S. dollar had perhaps the most to gain from the matter that has flowed—wars, oil, heroin and spilt blood—guns, oil, drugs and debt—from the mass murder in Manhattan on September 11, 2001.

Altoghether we'll see some harsh but vital realities ahead.

Since " '9/11' " we all have suffered from shocks and lies that degrade our capacities for reason and compassion. For decades and centuries before " '9/11' " we've been pushed into systems that exploit, degrade, and diminish us into sharing in criminality. We need now to wake up from the skein of scoundrels' schemes of which " '9/11' " is but the latest nightmare.

Closing this short book, we'll see alternatives that are now at work around the world—alternatives to the destructive, debt-based systems that endanger billions of us now—solutions that are spiritual as well as material and practical.

These cooperative solutions come from basic human feelings, concerns, and desires. Feelings of compassion. Concerns about posterity. Desires for more communication, more freedom, more pleasure, and more individual and collective accomplishment.

More life!

WTC 7

We were operating out of there when we were told that the World Trade Center was gonna collapse, and it did collapse before we could get out of the building.

Mayor Rudolph Giuliani speaks to ABC's Peter Jennings in the early afternoon of 9/11/01 about his temporary command center at 75 Barkley Street and the advance notice given to him of the unprecedented fall of the South Tower of the World Trade Center. [1]

It also may end up being a good investment. In the end, Mr. Silverstein may wind up controlling 11 million square feet of attractive, lower-rise modern space instead of 11 million square feet of 30-year-old space in New York's tallest and most conspicuous buildings.

The *Real Estate Journal* of the *Wall Street Journal* on 11/5/01 about one material gain to Silverstein Properties from the destruction of the World Trade Center's Twin Towers. The destruction of a third WTC skyscraper, Building 7, owned by Silverstein Properties and WTC 7's mortgage-holders (the Blackstone Group, General Motors Acceptance Corporation, and Banc of America Securities) on 9/11, resulted in an award of $861 million to those entities.

At 5:20 PM on September 11, 2001 a 47-story steel-framed skyscraper, World Trade Center Building 7, collapsed for no apparent reason in lower Manhattan of New York CIty.

Building 7 plunges into its footprint in a smooth, vertical motion.

In the minutes before its sudden but orderly fall, World Trade Center Building 7 showed only two small fires, burning on its 7th and 12th Floors, as aspects out of the ordinary in its structural appearance.

Never before or since 9/11/01 have fires of any size induced the collapse of a steel-framed high-rise building.

Due to some causal force, however, a force far beyond the heat of fires fueled by diesel or jet fuel or plastics, surface temperatures in the rubble of Building 7 and the Twin Towers registered more than 627°C (1161°F) five days after 9/11/01, according to the U.S. Geological Survey interpretation of National Aeronatics and Space Administration data, despite firefighters' regular soaking of these areas [2]

Building 7 around 5 PM.

WTC 7 was remarkably unscathed before its fall on 9/11/01. Sitting across Vesey Street on a northerly block which was separate from that of the six other World Trade Center Buildings, WTC 7 had escaped damage from the chunks of steel that were flung hundreds of feet outward when each of the 110-story Twin Towers, WTC 1 (the North Tower) and WTC 2 (the South Tower), fell so precipitously on the morning of 9/11/01.

WTC 7 was 300 feet from the nearest Twin Tower, the North Tower.

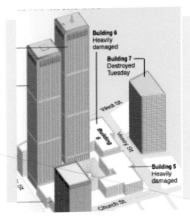

Maps of the World Trade Center before and after the Towers' collapses

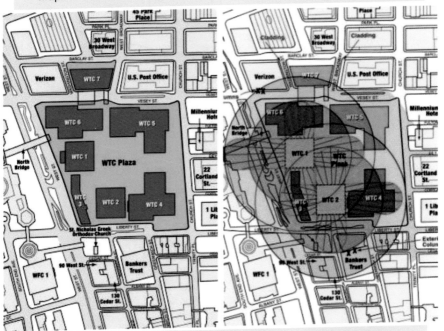

FEMA (the Federal Emergency Management Agency) documented the fallout pattern of the rubble from the Tower collapses. Heavy pieces of steel were ejected in all directions for distances up to 500 feet (dark orange regions) while aluminum cladding was blown up to 700 feet away from the Towers. The heavy steel fallout from the North Tower fell short of Vesey Street to the north, and far short of Building 7.

The collapse of WTC 7 shows many signs of controlled demolition.

First, this 47-story skyscraper, its height about five times its depth, dropped directly into its footprint in a smooth, vertical motion. The symmetry of WTC7's collapse meant that this Building's 58 perimeter columns and 25 central columns of structural steel must all have been shattered at almost the same instant.

Building 7 remains centered around its vertical axis as it falls.

Controlled demolition is required to achieve vertical collapse of structures much less tall than Building 7.

Second, WTC 7 collapsed completely in less than 7 seconds, a time almost equal to that of unimpeded free-fall. If a brick were dropped from 570 feet—the height of Building 7's roof—in a vacuum, it would hit the ground in 5.95 seconds. Thus, the building's falling mass encountered almost no resistance, showing that its structure had been destroyed before it fell.

This montage is composed of slices of frames from a CBS video of Building 7's collapse. The slices are separated by one-second intervals. The distance from the top of the intact building to the top of the logo is about 400 feet.

A third telltale feature of demolition is the dust that streamed out of the upper floors of Building 7 early in its collapse. These floors were far removed from the pockets of fire that had burned on the building's 7th and 12th floors. Such streamers are typical artifacts of the numerous small explosive charges used in a controlled demolition.

Streamers of dust emerge from the building's north facade.

A fourth sign of demolition is that WTC7's roof inverted toward its middle as the collapse progressed. This inversion and the fact that the mechanical penthouse dropped about a second before the facade indicate that the interior structure of the building was destroyed slightly ahead of the perimeter. Controlled demolitions are engineered in this manner to make tall buildings implode: as interior mass falls, it pulls the exterior inward.

This view from the north shows the center of Building 7 dropping slightly ahead of its outer edges, a signature of controlled demolitions.

A fifth characteristic of controlled demolition is shown by the shape of Building 7's rubble pile. WTC7's rubble was mostly confined to the block on which the building stood. The outer walls of this steel building ended up on the top of the pile, inwardly sloping to a height of not more than four stories.

Building 7's rubble pile was covered by its exterior walls.

The walls sloped inward toward the building's central axis.

This feature, like the inversion of the roof, indicates that the building's structures were shattered in a precise order, starting with interior elements, to implode the tall building and prevent it from toppling.

This aerial photo shows the remains of Building 7 piled up within the block it once occupied.

Only one adjacent building was significantly damaged by the collapse of the huge skyscraper. The two buildings closest to WTC 7, the U.S. Post Office building on the left, and the Verizon building on the right, were barely touched by the collapse. WTC 7's rubble pile continued to smolder for months.

Whereas Building 7 was converted to rubble lying mostly within its footprint, the destruction of the Twin Towers distributed their mass mostly outside their footprints.

The destruction of the the North Tower at 10:28 AM on 9/11/01 generated a rapidly expanding cloud of finely pulverized rubble that grew to many times the Tower's diameter as it raced down the building's vertical axis. Once the destruction reached the ground, this dense, pyroclastic cloud continued to grow upward and outward, expanding to about five times the building's volume within 30 seconds. The destruction of the South Tower 29 minutes earlier was nearly identical.

The vertical symmetry of the destruction of both Building 7 and the Twin Towers could only have been caused by controlled demolitions. The explosive pattern of destruction in the Towers, however, indicates that a far more energetic process was used to destroy them than to destroy Building 7.

The North Tower was consumed by an expanding cloud of dust that resembled a volcanic eruption.

In contrast to Building 7's consolidated rubble pile, the pulverized and shredded remains of the Twin Towers were dispersed far beyond their footprints over an area covering many blocks.

U.S. Government officials and news-media reports blamed fire for the collapse of WTC Building 7. Fire, however, has never been known to damage even a single column of a steel-framed skyscraper, let alone induce a collapse.

In 1991 fires at One Meridian Plaza in Philadelphia burned for 18 hours and gutted 8 floors of the 38-story building. All the steel columns and beams at One Merdian Plaza remained intact. The building was subsequently refurbished.

The One Meridian Plaza fire

In 1988 the First Interstate Bank Building in Los Angeles burned out-of-control for 3 1/2 hours, gutting 4 of this Tower's 62 floors. Afterward a company that analyzes the causes and effects of building fires, Iklim Ltd., reported:

> In spite of the total burnout of four and a half floors, there was no damage to the main structural members and only minor damage to one secondary beam and a small number of floor pans. [3]

The fires in these two skyscrapers were more severe than those in the three steel-framed World Trade Center buildings that totally collapsed.

The First Interstate Bank Building fire

The most comprehensive official investigation of the collapses of Building 7 and the Twin Towers—the most deadly and destructive structural failures of buildings in world history—was a study by a team of volunteers from the American Society of Civil Engineers whom the Federal Emergency Management Agency (FEMA) assembled in October 2001. The total budget for FEMA's Study was $600,000 —compared to $40 million spent by the U.S. government to investigate Bill Clinton's affair with Monica Lewinsky.

Other aspects of FEMA's Study were comparably inadequate or absurd.

Investigators were kept off the sites of the Buildings' collapses while evidence on these sites was hastily confiscated and destroyed. They lacked subpoena power and were prevented from obtaining blueprints for the buildings. The Science Committee of the House of Representatives later reported that ' the lack of authority of investigators to impound pieces of steel for investigation before they were recycled led to the loss of important pieces of evidence. ' [4]

In fact, the vast majority of the enduring fragments of steel columns from WTC 1, WTC 2 and WTC 7 were shipped to blast-furnaces in the Far East for melting without being seen by the investigators.

The structural steel from the three World Trade Center skyscrapers was rapidly removed from Ground Zero and the larger pieces shipped to blast furnaces in Asia. FEMA's volunteer investigators visited five salvage yards, starting about a month after the attack, and saved 156 pieces of steel for further study.

One contractor hired to dispose of evidence at the World Trade Center sites was Controlled Demolition, Inc., a Maryland-based company that was also responsible for the immediate confiscation and destruction of remains of the Murrah Federal Building in Oklahoma City after that building exploded, killing 168 people, on April 19, 1995.

Police found several unexploded bombs in the Murrah Building, a fact reported by several local TV news stations but not by national TV Networks. [5]

Retired Brigadier General Benton K. Partin, an expert in demolitions over his 31-year career in the U.S. Air Force, presented detailed proofs to the U.S. Congress in 1997 that the Murrah Building must have been demolished by internal explosives and not by an external truck-bomb. In June 1997 the U.S. Air Force Base in Eglin, Florida issued a 56-page 'Case Study' on the Murrah bombing that stated: " It must be concluded that the damage at the Murrah Federal Building is not the result of the truck bomb itself but rather due to other factors such as locally placed charges in the building itself. " [6]

The damage to the Murrah Building included a deep notch caused by the pulverization of a steel-reinforced concrete pillar. The blast pressure from the truck bomb on that pillar was only 27 pounds per square inch.

Congress and official investigators ignored both General Partin's and the Eglin Air Force Base Study's findings.

From October 2001 until the completion of their Study in May 2002 FEMA's scientific investigators were limited to off-site inspections of unidentified pieces of steel from WTC Buildings. Their only access to Ground Zero was a walk-through described as a "guided tour".

In January 2002 the 125-year-old publication Fire Engineering Magazine complained that the budget and limits of FEMA's 'Study' made it a ' half-baked farce '. [7]

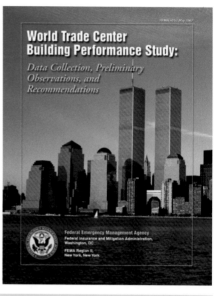

Undeterred by criticisms, however, FEMA in May 2002 issued the fruit of its $600,000-investigation of the unprecedented collapses that had cost more than 2000 lives, its Report #403, the *World Trade Center Building Performance Study*.

This Study contained many pages of cartoon-like schematics and misleading information and speculation. It also declined to be definitive. It wrote about the 'sequence of events' before the enormously deadly fall of each Twin Tower:

With the information and time available, the sequence of events leading to the collapse of each Tower could not be definitively determined.

The release of the FEMA Study coincided with the completion of the massive operation at Ground Zero to clean up and dispose of the evidence.

One of many deceptive illustrations in FEMA's report, this one from the chapter on WTC 7 implies that the building was adjacent to the collapsed Towers by superimposing 'WTC COMPLEX' and 'Collapse of WTC 1' on the northerly portion of the World Trade Center super-block. In fact, Building 7 was separated from the nearest Tower by 300 feet.

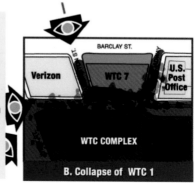

FEMA's 'World Trade Center Building Performance Study' is even more non-committal in regard to the fall of WTC 7. It wrote in conclusion:

> The specifics of the fires in WTC 7 and the how they caused the building to collapse remain unknown at this time. Although the total diesel fuel on the premises contained massive potential energy, the best hypothesis has only a low probability of occurrence. Further research, investigation, and analyses are needed to resolve this issue.

No further research is needed, however, to show that only a controlled demolition could have caused the symmetric collapse of World Trade Center Building 7.

Some of FEMA's volunteer investigators examine some steel in a salvage yard. The Study gives three reasons that only 156 pieces of steel were saved for further study:

- Some pieces were later determined not to be relevant to understanding building damage.
- Once a coupon was taken, the full piece was discarded.
- Pieces were accidentally processed in salvage yard operations before they were removed from the yards for further study.

A question arises from the obvious demolition of WTC 7: Why destroy such a valuable piece of real estate?

We know that WTC7's developer and lease-holder, Silverstein Properties, and WTC7's mortgage-holders, the Blackstone Group, Banc of America Securities, and General Motors Acceptance Corporation, received a Court-awarded amount of $861 million dollars from Industrial Risk Insurers in February 2002. We know that about $386 million had been invested in WTC7 before its destruction. The Court-award meant that Silverstein Properties and the mortgage-holders would share in about $475 million of profit. [8]

Silverstein Properties is headed by Larry Silverstein, a large contributor to Democrat and Republican office-holders. Silverstein Properties became the primary owner of the WTC Twin Towers less than two months before 9/11/01 (Westfield

Standing just north of the WTC complex, Building 7 was one of the larger buildings in Manhattan.

Malls was Silverstein Properties' minority-partner). Buying from the New York Port Authority, Silverstein Properties invested only $15 million toward a total purchase-price of $3.2 billion for a 99-year lease on holdings worth an estimated $8 billion. The low-rise office buildings WTC 4, 5, and 6, and 400,000 square feet of retail space were included with the Twin Towers in this deal. Silverstein Properties immediately took out extensive insurance policies on its new holdings.

One clause in Silverstein Properties' insurance policies for the new WTC holdings soon proved instrumental. Quoting the British *Financial Times* of September 14, 2001, the *American Reporter* wrote that ' the lease has an all-important escape clause: If the buildings are struck by "an act of terrorism", the new owners' obligations under the lease are void. As a result, the new owners are not required to make any payments under their lease, but they will be able to collect on the loss of the buildings that collapsed or were otherwise destroyed and damaged in the attacks. ' [9] Silverstein Properties is still contesting the amount of pay-out due for destruction of the Twin Towers—$3.55 billion for one 'occurrence' or $7.1 billion for two 'occurrences'. The "terrorism" clause in his lease has given Larry Silverstein leverage in negotiating his new deal for the site. [10]

In addition to offices of the Securities and Exchange Commission, the CIA, the Department of Defense, the Secret Service, and the IRS, World Trade Center Building 7 held an Emergency Command Center for the City of New York that Mayor Rudolph Giuliani had built in professed response to the bombing of the Twin Towers by supposed "Muslim extremists" on February 20, 1993. [11]

Completed in 1997, Giuliani's Command Center on the 23rd floor of WTC 7 had walls and windows built to withstand bombs and bullets and 160-miles-per-hour winds as well as its own supplies of oxygen and water.

On the morning of 9/11/01's airliner-strikes to the Twin Towers, Mayor Giuliani went not to his Command Center—with its clear view of the Twin Towers—but to a makeshift, street-level headquarters at 75 Barkley Street.

He and staff fled this location when they were told that the South Tower was going to collapse, Giuliani told ABC's Peter Jennings in the early afternoon of 9/11/01. " We were operating out of there when we were told that the World Trade Center was gonna collapse, " Giuliani said, " and it did collapse before we could get out of the building. "

How Giuliani could be warned of a collapse that was not anticipated even by firefighters inside the South Tower (see the talk of deceased New York Fire Department Batallion Chief Orio J. Palmer on page 24), is one of many questions about Government officials' behavior on 9/11/01.

Certain, however, is that total demolition of WTC 7 would be the surest means of destroying evidence that its Emergency Command Center was the command-center for the greatest single act of mass murder against U.S. civilians ever.

Giuliani's fortified Emergency Command Center on Building 7's 23rd floor provided an unobstructed view of the entire height of both Twin Towers. Also, Building 7 straddled a ConEd electrical substation that provided power for most of Lower Manhattan—including the entire World Trade Center.

Certain too, is that WTC 7's Emergency Command Center offered a perfect, protected vantage from which to execute the demolition of each Twin Tower.

In September of 2002 the United States' Public Broadcasting System aired a documentary about construction at the World Trade Center complex that was entitled "America Rebuilds". [12]

In this one-hour documentary Larry Silverstein spoke about tumultuous events on 9/11/01. He revealed a decision about World Trade Center Building 7 that was apparently unnoticed by mass media or by the entity that had agreed to pay $861 million the previous February for the loss of

AMERICA REBUILDS
· a year at ground zero ·

From the unimaginable horror of the September 11 attacks arose new tests of American character and ingenuity. As engineers, firefighters and workers heroically cleared Ground Zero, a diverse group of New Yorkers have struggled toward consensus for the site's future.

WTC 7, Industrial Risk Insurers. His revelation should have struck like a bombshell of front-and-center news the next day. Larry Silverstein said:

I remember getting a call from the, er, fire department commander, telling me that they were not sure they were gonna be able to contain the fire, and I said, " We've had such terrible loss of life, maybe the smartest thing to do is pull it ". And they made that decision to pull and we watched the building collapse.

In the context of its repeated usage by Silverstein here, pull means to demolish. That is, the 70-year-old mogul stated on national television that in accord with his advice the New York Fire Department had deliberately destroyed Building 7. His statement can be heard at www.wtc7.net/pullit/ .

The "pulling" of Building 7 emptied the city block it occupied without seriously affecting adjacent real-estate.

Since 9/11/01 Silverstein Properties has argued with WTC 7's mortgage-holders (the Blackstone Group, GMAC, and Banc of America Securities) about the amount of office-space and consequent revenue that the new building on the site should provide. The mortgage-holders want 1.9 million square-feet of office-space instead of Silverstein Properties' proposed 1.6 million.

Why was Silverstein's claim of an incredibly expeditious demolition not headline (MOGUL ADMITS 9/11 BUILDING DEMOLISHED) news? Because news of Silverstein's claim would have awoken people to the likelihood that the Twin Towers also were demolished.

Silverstein's claim itself is absurd. It asks us to believe that hundreds of charges were placed throughout the supposedly dangerous Building 7 within a few hours, then detonated with precise timing, to produce the subsequent, symmetric, vertical collapse.

Why was Silverstein's claim uttered at all? Because the demolition of WTC 7 was so obvious and becoming so widely known that it needed an explanation— a fallback story, a cover story—however incredible that explanation was and is.

Let's consider how broadly incriminating Silverstein's statement is. If we acknowledge that the symmetric demolition of WTC 7 could only have happened through the emplacement of internal explosives on floors of this Building from basement to roof before 9/11/01, we must then suppose that principals among the Buildings' owners, its mortgage-holders and office-holders, at least knew about such an extensive emplacement.

We can now begin to see more deeply into the plot behind the mass murder on 9/11/01. We can see that 'al Quada' could not have carried out the demolition of even one World Trade Center Building. We can begin to see who must have been principal and integral to the crimes of " '9/11' " and their even more murderous consequences. Larry Silverstein is a rather large player within the realms of 21st-century real estate, finance, and politics, but much more powerful financiers than he are now profiting from " '9/11' "—just as history of the Western world shows that the same families of financiers have profited

The devastation of the World Trade Center, blamed on Osama bin Ladin, enriched financiers, boosted politicians' fortunes, and supplied a pretext for U.S. imperial ventures.

from prior pretexts for war. These pretexts have deceived hundreds of thousands within the U.S. and tens of millions worldwide into dying for cruelly illusory causes.

The Twin Towers

Whereas the destruction of Building 7 remains little-known, hidden behind silence and absurdities, the destruction of the Twin Towers is still the centerpiece of of the manufactured terror of the 9/11/01 attack. The success of the Big Lie that the Twin Towers collapsed due to collision and fire-induced stress is in part attributable to the accuracy and realism of one much-repeated aspect of the Official Story—UA 175's crash into the South Towers. The spectacular fireball of the South Tower crash—the appalling awesomeness of this moment—draws attention away from the true cause of the collapses.

We begin our examination of the core event of the 9/11/01 attack—the massacre in Lower Manhattan—by reviewing the generally accepted account of the Tower crashes.

The North Tower was hit at 8:46 AM EDT by American Airlines Flight 11, a Boeing 767 that had departed Boston's Logan Airport at 7:58 that morning. [1] This airliner drove squarely into the northeast side of WTC 1 while banked at an angle of about 25 degrees. Flight 11 directly impacted portions of Floors 94 through 98 and broke through 31 to 36 of the 59 perimeter columns on this side of the building, according to FEMA's Study.

Flight 11 was traveling about 470 miles per hour at impact. It left a rough, cookie-cutter outline of its tilting shape. Fires from exploding jet fuel, atomized by the collision, broke out immediately on portions of the impacted floors.

The crash of Flight 11, a 767, into the North Tower left an impression of the jet out to the wingtips and end of the tail.

At 9:03 AM, 17 minutes after the North Tower impact, United Airlines Flight 175, another Boeing 767 that had departed Boston's Logan Airport, struck the South Tower less directly. This airliner hit WTC 2 toward the Tower's southeast corner between Floors 78 and 84. Much of UA 175's load of jet-fuel (which is essentially kerosene) exploded in a fireball outside the Tower.

Flight 175's fireball

In contrast to the centered North Tower impact, the South Tower impact was oblique, producing far less damage to the building and largely sparing its stout core structure.

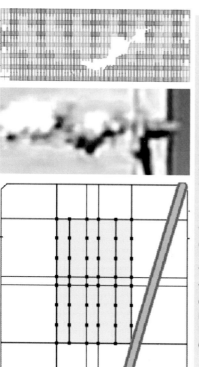

The South Tower's impact hole shows that the plane's fuselage entered the right end of the middle third of the Tower's southeast wall, and a video shows a portion of it exiting the Tower's east corner. This indicates that the plane's fuselage almost missed the entire core structure (which retained at least one passable stairwell after the crash). The graphic shows the probable trajectory of the fuselage (brown) relative to the core structure (orange).

Damage to the South Tower's perimeter wall consisted of the severing of about 23 of its 240 perimeter columns.

Thus the impact of Flight 175 damaged less than 10 percent of the South Tower's columns and damaged them only in a region between the 78th and 84th floors. Its puncture of the far corner allowed much of the jet fuel to escape into the fireball.

The two Towers burned and stood for much different lengths of time after they were hit by Boeing 767s.

The North Tower stood for 102 minutes after its direct impact from Flight 11, while the South Tower stood for 56 minutes after its oblique impact from Flight 175.

The reason most frequently given to explain the much longer persistence of the North Tower is that the greater mass above the South Tower's crash zone caused it to collapse first. Several facts contradict this explanation.

First, the structural damage to the South Tower was far less severe. Fewer of its perimeter columns were damaged and very few of its core columns were compromised.

Second, the fires in the South Tower were far less severe, as much of UA Flight 175's fuel exited the building. While the North Tower continued to emit prodigious smoke, the South Tower was producing only a thin veil of black smoke by the time of its collapse. Black smoke indicates cooling, oxygen-starved fires.

Flames were visible in the South Tower (right) for only a few minutes after the impact. They never spread beyond the impact zone and they appeared to diminish over time.

By the time of the South Tower's collapse, its smoke was thin and black.

Finally, the tapering of the thickness of the steel comprising the Towers' 47 core box columns and 240 perimeter box columns from ground to roof-level meant that the columns were about twice as strong at the South Tower's 80th floor impact zone as at the North Tower's 95th floor impact zone.

Fire within the South Tower appeared so manageable that New York Fire Department Battalion Chief Orio J. Palmer asked for more engines and firefighters at 9:48 EDT, 11 minutes before this Tower began to explode. Having reached the 78th floor Sky Lobby with Fire Marshal Ronald P. Bucca, Palmer reported " two pockets of fire ". [2]

Chief Orio J. Palmer

Battalion 7 Chief: Battalion Seven ... Ladder 15, we've got two isolated pockets of fire. We should be able to knock it down with two lines. Radio that, 78th floor numerous 10-40 Code Ones.

...

Ladder 15: Floor 78?

Battalion 7 Chief: Ten-four, numerous civilians, we gonna need two engines up here.

...

Battalion 7 Chief: I'm going to need two of your firefighters Adam, stairway to knock down two fires. We have house line stretched we could use some water on it, knock it down, kay.

Other workers reported evidence of bombs on the 9/11/01 morning. 51-year-old firefighter Louie Caachioli was quoted in the *People Weekly* of 9/24/02 about his experience in the South Tower:

I was taking firefighters up in the elevator to the 24th floor to get in position to evacuate workers. On the last trip up a bomb went off. We think there were bombs set in the building.

Stationary engineer Mike Pecoraro was shaken by an explosion in the 6th sub-basement of the North Tower. Climbing to Level C of the basement, Pecoraro found a machine shop and its 50-ton hydraulic press both " gone! ", reduced to rubble, he told *Chief Engineer* magazine. He saw a ' line of smoke streaming through the air ' on level C. He climbed to Level B, one floor below the North Tower's lobby, and saw ' a steel and concrete fire door that weighed about 300 pounds '. He described this door as wrinkled up " like a piece of aluminum foil ". [3]

No network coverage of the horror in New York City that morning noted such obvious evidence of explosion and demolition. None said that the Towers had "exploded". None said "demolition". Instead, mass-media outlets immediately began to promote explanations that some combination of impact trauma and fire stress caused the collapses. [4]

Three such distinct explanations appeared. While all are absurd, the second and third theories employed scenarios of increasing complexity to hide their underlying nonsense.

The first Official Explanation to be broadcast was that fires ignited by the jetliners' fuel had melted steel beams and columns within the Towers and thus caused the skyscrapers to 'collapse'.

The British Broadcasting Company quoted 'structural engineer' Chris Wise in its September 13, 2001 piece *How the World Trade Center Fell*. Wise spoke with cinematic emphasis:

> It was the fire that killed the buildings. There's nothing on earth that could survive those temperatures with that amount of fuel burning ... The columns would have melted, the floors would have melted and eventually they would have collapsed one on top of each other.

The BBC online news story of 9/13/01 also quoted another expert. The buildings' construction manager, Hyman Brown, agreed that nothing could have saved them from the inferno.

The buildings would have stood had a plane or a force caused by a plane smashed into it, But steel melts, and 24,000 gallons of aviation fluid melted the steel. Nothing is designed or will be designed to withstand that fire. [5]

This graphic from the BBC is thoroughly inaccurate.

- It describes the columns as steel-reinforced concrete when in fact they were 100% steel.
- It depicts the core as a being a fraction of its actual dimensions.
- It states that 800° C temperatures can melt steel, when steel's melting point is 1535° C.

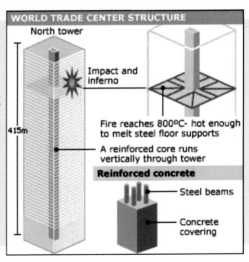

WORLD TRADE CENTER STRUCTURE

North tower

415m

Impact and inferno

Fire reaches 800ºC- hot enough to melt steel floor supports

A reinforced core runs vertically through tower

Reinforced concrete

Steel beams

Concrete covering

The fundamental problem with the jet-fuel-melting-steel explanation is that its premise contradicts the laws of physics. No amount of ' "aviation fluid" ' burning in the open flames of a building fire could even begin to melt steel. 1535° Celsius is the melting point of structural steel, whereas 825° Celsius is around the maximum temperature attainable with hydrocarbon-fueled fires burning in the air without systematic pre-heating or pressurization of the air.

The second explanation for the Twin Towers' fall is that the vertical columns were heated to the point of buckling and collapse. This theory was first articulated by Professor Jacques Bazant and graduate assistant Young Zhou in a paper, *Why Did the World Trade Center Collapse--Simple Analysis* published in the *Journal of Engineering Mechanics* on 9/13/01. [6]

Bazant's and Zhou's remarkably swift explanation advances one basic premise as cause for the collapses while offering a disclaimer that invalidates its entire premise and explanation. It states that all the columns on one floor of each Tower simultaneously sustained temperatures exceeding 800° C. It makes this statement as its basic premise despite overwhelming evidence to the contrary. Photographs and video footage from 9/11/01 show none of the features of widespread fires exceeding even 700° C—such as ongoing window breakage; large, bright, emergent flames; and light-colored smoke.

Further, temperatures of the steel columns must have remained far below fire temperatures. Since steel is an excellent conductor of heat, and the tens of thousands of tons of steel comprising the Towers' columns were well-connected, heat absorbed by columns in areas of fire was rapidly wicked away to other parts of the massive structures. Had any of the exterior columns been heated to 700° C, they would have glowed red-hot.

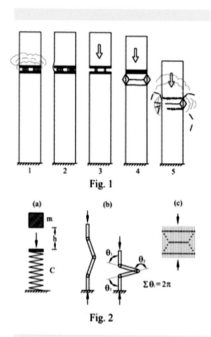

Bazant and Zhou used 'elastic dynamic analysis' to assert that one story's collapse in each Tower meant that the building was 'doomed'.

A maker of car parks in Europe, Corus Construction, subjected steel-framed car parks to full-scale fire tests, fueled by hydrocarbon fuels similar to jet fuel, in the U.S., the United Kingdom, Japan, and Australia. The highest temperature that these tests registered in any of the steel beams and columns was 360° C. [7]

Bazant and Zhou's '*Simple Analysis*' somehow survived as the basis for Silverstein Properties' claim of $7.2 billion from Credit Reinsurance for the Towers' fall.

The third and most broadcast of mass media explanations for the Towers' destruction was one championed by Dr. Thomas Eagar, a Materials Science Professor at the Massachusetts Institute of Technology.

Eagar's analysis was first published in the *Journal of the Minerals, Metals and Materials Society*. [8] It blames alleged failures of lightweight open floor trusses for the total collapse of the Twin Towers. Hence it's called the "truss-failure theory". Eagar cleverly disguises the absurdities of his theory by preceding outright lies with facts. For example, Eagar likens the Towers' columns to rows of dominoes after stating the truth that engineers employ highly redundant designs.

Eagar's deceptive techniques exhibit greater refinement in a subsequent interview broadcast by NOVA. [9] Here he adds zippers to dominoes in his repertoire of metaphors. He asserts that failure of the 'angle clips' — his misnomer for the steel shelves that supported the ends of the trusses — precipitated an 'unzipping' chain reaction of truss failures. Such, he asserts, led to a 'pancaking' chain reaction of floor failures.

Once you started to get angle clips to fail in one area, it put extra load on other angle clips, and then it **unzipped** around the building on that floor in a matter of seconds.

Eagar suggests that the floors supported the columns instead of the opposite, obvious reality: the columns supported the floors.

A graphic from NOVA's website shows only parallel trusses, omitting both the perpendicular cross-trusses and the floor pans which unified the floor structures.

This schematic from NOVA's site depicts the core structure as horizontal slabs instead of vertical columns. It subliminally reinforces the idea that the Towers' could easily "pancake".

Despite its intrinsic falsity, Eagar's theory was largely adopted by FEMA's $600,000 *World Trade Center Building Performance Study*.

The FEMA engineers' Study also misrepresents the Towers' construction. Their central deception is to misrepresent the Towers' stout structural cores as 'service cores' by using misleading language and deceptive illustrations such as the two shown here.

A rectangular **service core** with overall dimensions of approximately 87 feet by 137 feet, was present at the center of each building, housing 3 exit stairways, 99 elevators, and 16 escalators.

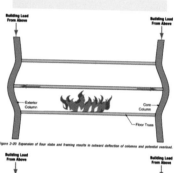

Figure 2-20 Expansion of floor slabs and framing results in outward deflection of columns and potential overload.

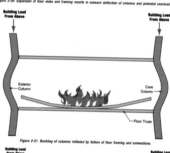

Figure 2-21 Buckling of columns initiated by failure of floor framing and connections.

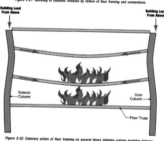

Figure 2-22 Catenary action of floor framing on several floors initiates column buckling failures.

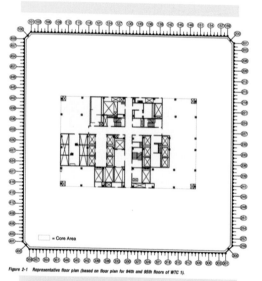

Figure 2-1   Representative floor plan (based on floor plan for 94th and 95th floors of WTC 1).

☐ = Core Area

This floor plan reinforces the idea that the Towers' 'service cores' had no significant structural function, misrepresenting the core columns (red squares) as only a fraction of their actual dimensions. Nowhere does the report show the core's cross-bracing beams.

The fine print in this illustration reveals that it represents a section of a Tower extending from a perimeter wall to the edge of the core. To the casual reader, however, it appears to represent the entire span between opposite perimeter walls and thus implies that the Towers had no core structures.

Construction photographs of the Twin Towers reveal a possible reason FEMA went to such great lengths to hide the existence of the structural cores.

Each Tower's core contained 47 continuous box-columns which ran from the bedrock foundations seven stories below street level to near the tops of the Towers, where they transitioned to I-beams. These box-columns measured 36 inches by 16 inches and were fabricated of steel four inches thick near the Towers' bases.

FEMA's report hides and minimizes the core structures whose existence made the symmetric total collapses of the Towers due to gravity impossible. Even if the collision and fire damage could have induced collapse events, they would have caused the Towers to topple like trees, pivoting about the cores at the impact zones.

This construction photograph of the North Tower shows that the core structures consisted of bundles of columns cross-linked by horizontal and diagonal members.

Destroying the core columns is key to achieving total building collapse. And yet FEMA's report has only one short passage explaining how the cores self-destructed.

As the floors collapsed, this left tall freestanding portions of the exterior wall and possibly central core columns. As the unsupported height of these freestanding exterior wall elements increased, they buckled at the bolted column splice connections, and also collapsed.

Note the legalistic language of ' *possibly* central core columns '. The authors knew the core columns were not free-standing and would not instantly self-destruct if the floors fell away. Nor were the perimeter columns free-standing, as the passage implies; they were stitched together by horizontal spandrell plates. By qualifying this key assertion, FEMA's team might have been protecting themselves from possible future prosecution.

Both Professor Eagar and FEMA present a scenario that starts with truss failures and culminates in total building collapse. Both present their scenario's initial events in some detail and grow ever vaguer as they play their scenario out. The detail and complexity in their theory's initial stages serves to distract from the glaring contradictions that evidence exposes about their theory's latter stages.

Said evidence includes many photographs and videos that show the progression of each Tower's destruction from widely different vantage points. Through this extensive, self-corroborating body of evidence we see that that each collapse commenced in an instant and proceeded to total destruction of each building in under 16 seconds. We see that the Towers' columns did not buckle at the onsets of the collapses. Rather, each Tower's top plunged into a burgeoning cloud of thick dust and rubble, a cloud that exploded continuously in all directions at over 40 feet per second as it descended, expanding to a radius of up to 500 feet before reaching the ground.

The above series of photographs shows the South Tower at about 5, 5.9, and 7.5 seconds after its top started to fall. Times were determined through comparing features in photos of the exploding dust cloud to the same features in videos of the South Tower's collapse. Using the Tower's width of 207 feet as a yardstick, it's easy to see that the rate of the cloud's expansion is about 50 feet per second between the first and second photographs and about 80 feet per second between the second and third photographs.

People frequently assume that only structural engineers are qualified to draw conclusions about what destroyed the Towers. But there are many common-sense proofs that the Towers were destroyed by controlled demolition. The following arguments meet the standard of proof used in criminal trials.

PROOF 1: The Towers fell through themselves with dead-centered symmetry.

The collapses remained centered around the Towers' vertical axes as they raced to the ground. That is, the collapses followed what would have been the path of *maximal resistance* unless the structure was being demolished ahead of the falling mass. But physical processes follow the path of *least resistance*. Thus, tall structures topple instead of crushing themselves. Without controlled demolition, the Towers' tops would have toppled, leaving standing their portions below the impact zones.

The South Tower's destruction began with its top tipping to the southeast. Instead of toppling, however, the top suddenly disintegrated and fell into the exploding Tower. By eight seconds (pictured) the event had become quite symmetric.

The North Tower's destruction was symmetrical from its onset, when the top ten stories began to telescope. By three seconds the North Tower's top had disappeared, and by eight seconds (pictured) it was rapidly mushrooming.

PROOF 2: Non-metallic materials were pulverized to fine dust in the air.

Most of the non-metallic components and contents of the Towers were converted to fine dust *in mid-air*. Photographs and accounts from Ground Zero confirm that what was left of the Towers consisted of the shredded remains of the Towers' steel skeletons, other metallic remnants, paper, and fine dust. There is a striking absence of evidence of macroscopic pieces of concrete from the approximately 90,000 tons of concrete that constituted the four-inch-thick floor slabs of each Tower, or of shards of glass from the over 25,000 panes of plate glass that enveloped each Tower. Analysis of powder samples shows that the concrete, glass, gypsum, and fiberglass insulation were converted to a homogeneous mixture of dust, mostly consisting of sub-100-micron particles. [10]

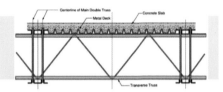

The three million cubic feet of concrete comprising the Towers' floor slabs was pulverized to fine powder.

Videos and photographs of the Towers' collapses as well as the accompanying dust cloud's fallout pattern show that pulverization of concrete and other materials began early in each collapse, when each Tower's top was falling only tens of feet per second relative to the standing portion of the building.

Proponents of the Official Explanations for the collapses describe a " pile-driver effect ". Said effect has the Towers' portions above their impact zones smashing the lower floors as they descend. Again, however, photographs and vidoes show that the Towers' portions above their impact zones *disintegrated* into rubble in less than 4.5 and 3 seconds during the South and North Towers' collapses respectively.

Dense clouds of concrete were apparent early in each collapse.

Thus the material that might make for a "pile-driver effect" exploded into rubble which could not possibly pulverize concrete into powder.

Neither could the thorough pulverization of the concrete have been caused by ground impact. A block of concrete dropped from a height of 1360 feet would shatter into small pieces, but would not be reduced to microscopic particles.

PROOF 3: The North Tower disappeared as rapidly as rubble falling through air.

The Towers disappeared into exploding dust clouds that first consumed their falling tops and then consumed their remaining structures from top to bottom in about 15 seconds as they plummeted to ground. Each Tower's dust cloud grew to several times the building's diameter within a few seconds, so that the majority of each Tower's material was falling freely through the air outside the former building's profile. Materials falling outside its profile were slowed only by air resistance, but materials falling inside its profile would hve been slowed further by the building's solid structure below. And yet, no portion of either Tower remained standing above the descending rubble cloud.

At 8.5 seconds into its collapse the top of the North Tower's cloud of dust and steel fragments was falling at about 50 feet per second both inside and outside the Tower's profile.

This proves that the falling rubble was not crushing the Tower.

Air resistance slowed the descent of the rubble outside the building's profile by about 50 percent compared to the rate of free-fall in a vacuum. But the over 1000 vertical feet of intact structure did not slow portions falling within the profile any more than air. This can be verified by examining the top of the North Tower's dust cloud, which is essentially the same height both inside and outside the building's profile.

Each Tower was supported by a lattice of 90,000 tons of steel strong enough to resist earthquakes and hurricane-force winds. To believe the Official Story requires one to think that these immensely strong structures provided no more resistance to falling rubble than did air.

PROOF 4: The South Tower's top disintegrated before falling.

The South Tower's collapse began with its extent above the crash zone appearing to tip to the southeast, the direction of the corner most damaged by the impact of UA 175. It appears to tilt toward this corner. However, close examination shows that the top (the above-impact portion) doesn't pivot about the crash zone. Rather, it starts to bend and then disintegrates from the crash zone upward, destroying structure *before* it falls into the intact structure below. Hence it's obvious that the top was being destroyed by some force other than gravity-driven crushing.

That the South Tower's top shattered and exploded ahead of collapsing into itself is demonstrated by two separate features. First, photographs show the edges of the Tower between the 80th to the 100th floors bending in a long arc as the top began to fall. Since the Towers were made of steel rather than rubber, this can only be explained by the thorough destruction of structures throughout that area.

Curved walls mean structure was shattered tens of stories above the supposed zone of crushing.

A second feature is the disappearance of angular momentum in the falling top. As the top first began to tip, its rotation accelerated as if it was beginning to topple, pivoting about a point in the impact zone. However, as the top then began to fall, the rotation decelerated. Then it reversed direction. The law of conservation of angular momentum states that a solid object in rotation will continue to rotate at the same speed unless acted on by a torque. As the top tilted to the southeast the only torque—provided by the resistance of the bottom— should have caused the top to rotate faster in the same direction. Why then did it stop rotating before disappearing into the dust cloud? This behavior is reconciled with the laws of physics by understanding that as the top disintegrated from the bottom up, so did its moment of inertia, converting the angular momentum of that block of thirty stories into linear momentum of pieces of rubble.

A video montage showing the South Tower's collapse at one-second intervals. View the video at http://9-11research.com/videos/ to see the reversal of the top's rotation.

PROOF 5: The energy required to destroy the Towers and expand the ensuing dust clouds far exceeded officially acknowledged supplies.

The collapses of the Twin Towers involved conversions of vast amounts of energy. According to the laws of physics, energy can be converted between different forms, but it cannot be created or destroyed. Therefore, all the energy expended in the collapses of the Towers (energy sinks) had to come from forms of potential energy extant at their outset (energy sources). The energy sinks included the following physical processes:

- Shredding of the steel skeletons
- Pulverization of concrete and glass into fine powder
- Acceleration of the mass outward up to 500 feet in all directions
- Ground shaking of the magnitude 2 earthquake produced by each collapse
- Expansion of the dust cloud following each collapse to several times the Tower's size within seconds

The South Tower's dust cloud advanced down the streets of Lower Manhattan at about 30 miles per hour.

According to the Official Story, the energy source driving all of this destruction was the gravitational potential energy of the Towers' elevated mass. That quantity is easily computed by multiplying the mass of each Tower by its average elevation. That quantity amounts to about 110 megawatt hours per Tower.

Estimating the magnitudes of the energy sinks is less straightforward, given the large gaps in quantitative data about the collapses. However, it is possible to compute the lower bounds of the dust cloud expansion energy sink with some certainty. Such is the objective of Jim Hoffman's paper *The North Tower's Dust Cloud: Analysis of Energy Requirements for the Expansion of the Dust Cloud Following the Collapse of 1 World Trade Center.* Based on the photograph on page 11, he estimates that the North Tower's dust cloud had grown to at least five times the volume of the Tower 30 seconds after it started to collapse. Ignoring the possibility that explosives helped to expand the clouds, it concludes that the expansion would have come mainly from a combination of vaporization of water in the building and increases in temperatues of gases and suspended solids. Its most conservative estimate for total energy inputs is 1,600 megawatt hours. [11]

So: even if we overlook all the other energy sinks in the North Tower's destruction, merely expanding its dust clouds took over ten times the energy of the only acknowledged energy source.

Now—following many pages of close analyses—we're done with the debunking of the Official Explanations. Now we're done with proofs that WTC Buildings 1, 2, and 7 were destroyed by controlled demolition on 9/11/01.

Now we can answer as to the crimes of 9/11/01 in New York City, the What of investigators' What—When—Where—Who—How—Why template. We also know, of course, the When and Where of these crimes. We may reasonably suppose the How of these crimes, too, while acknowledging that the destruction of the Twin Towers exceeds the capacities of forces and methods known to the lay public.

We still have to address Who and Why.

Who and Why return us return to the realm of individual human beings, their motives and morality. We return to the over 2,750 dead in New York City on 9/11/01, over 2,600 of them not aboard either crashed airliner, over 2,000 of them workers in the Twin Towers, 479 of them public-service personnel, including 343 firefighters. [12]

The Who of the dead includes wives and husbands, sons and daughters, fathers and mothers, cousins, aunts and uncles, along with friends and friends of friends beyond numbering.

The forces that destroyed the Twin Towers also destroyed the remains of the victims to a degree that made the identification of most of their bodies difficult or impossible. Few victims were identified in the first weeks, leaving survivors with forlorn hopes that their loved ones might still be alive. A year after the attack over one thousand victims remained unidentified. [13]

Why so many of these people died as we must now know they did die—through the calculated demolition of each of the Twin Towers; that is, through cold-blooded mass murder—leads us to the inescapable contemplation of who had the likeliest means, motive, and opportunity to carry out these crimes, crimes so immoral or amoral that they're beyond the imagining (' The bigger the lie, therefore, the likelier it is to be believed. ') of ordinary and compassionate human beings.

The Financiers Behind " '9/11' "

Actor-cum-politician Arnold Schwarzenegger, son of an Austrian Nazi, with financiers Warren Buffet and Jacob Rothschild at Rothschild's English estate on 9/16/02. Rothschild interests are widely said to control the United States' central Bank, the Federal Reserve System. [1]

If the American people ever allow private banks to control the issue of currency, first by inflation, then by deflation, the banks and corporations that will grow up around them will deprive the people of all property until their children wake up homeless on the continent their fathers conquered.

President Thomas Jefferson to Secretary of the Treasury Albert Gallatin, 1802 [2]

If the Council on Foreign Relations raises the hackles of conspiracy theorists, the Bilderberg meetings must induce apocalyptic visions of omnipotent international bankers plotting with unscrupulous government officials to impose cunning schemes on an ignorant and unsuspecting world.

David Rockefeller, financier to Nazis after World War II, former Chairman of the Chase Manhattan Bank and of the Council on Foreign Relations, writing facetiously in his 2002 <u>Memoirs</u> [3]

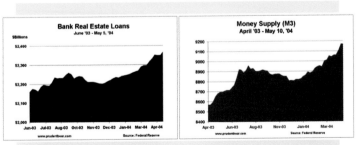

Mountains of debt from institutions threaten the U.S. public.

Parts One and Two of our book have conclusively shown, we hope, that the World Trade Center's Building 7 and Twin Towers must have been demolished by internal explosives on September 11, 2001.

These demolitions, we believe, must have been carried out by a secret team whose operations were known within the United States Government. No other explanation answers all the facts about the destruction of the three WTC Buildings.

We're thus confronted with the awful likelihood that some power within the United States Government—some power perhaps above the United States Government—executed or allowed the mass murder of more than 2,750 civilians in New York City on 9/11/01.

Why was this horrific crime committed? By examining who and what profited from the attacks of September 11, 2001 we may see possible reasons for the mass murder on that day and the consequent deaths of many more thousands of people due to the " 'War on Terror' " in Afghanistan and Iraq.

We can see for certain that many of the same entities which benefited from destruction of WTC 7 and the Twin Towers are also profiting from the ongoing wars in Afghanistan and Iraq and from threats to nations' domestic security.

In the pages ahead we'll also see that the largest beneficiaries of " '9/11' " and the " 'War on Terror' " are corporations that profit from trade in oil and gas, armaments, and usury. These same corporations, controlled by a few banks, also profit from more than $180 billion per year in sales of opium-unto-heroin from Afghanistan. Their four main supports make up an acronym of G.O.D.D. (Guns, Oil, Drugs, Debt). Their overall intention appears to be global control known for decades as the 'New World Order'.

The crisis in the Persian Gulf, as grave as it is, also offers a rare opportunity to move toward an historic period of cooperation. Out of these troubled times, our fifth objective—a new world order—can emerge ...

George H. W. Bush to a joint session of Congress, 9/11/90 [4]

There is a chance for the President of the United States to use this disaster to carry out ... a phrase his father used ... and that is a New World Order.

Gary Hart, former Senator from Colorado, speaking at the General Meeting of the Council on Foreign Relations on 9/14/02. Hart's fellow CFR panelists were Warren Rudman, Newt Gingrich, and Lee Hamilton. Lee Hamilton was later co-chair of the National Commission on Terrorist Attacks. [5]

We 'll also see that banks are ultimately making the most money from " '9/11' " and the " 'War on Terror' " at the same time as we'll see that the United States' most major banks needed an event such as " '9/11' " and its subsequent wars to save their system from collapse. We'll see that many of the chief executives of the banks and other corporations that have most profited from " '9/11' " also were or are integral to the World Trade Center complex.

Finally, we'll see that these banks and the few families who control them have manipulated the masses of the United States and the world into Wars, Depressions and other means of mass murder and misery for more than a century to increase their power and profits. The 'New World Order' that they presume to impose on us makes horrors such as " '9/11' " inevitable.

We know that the Blackstone Group became a mortgage-holder for World Trade Center Building 7 in October 2000, 11 months before the demolitions of 9/11/01, and that the Blackstone Group is expected to share with Silverstein Properties, Banc of America Securities and the General Motors Acceptance Corporation in the hundreds of millions of dollars from insurance payments that are related to the WTC 7 site.

Peter G. Peterson

The Blackstone Group is an investment-banking firm begun by Peter A. Peterson and Stephen Schwartzman in 1985, the same year that a similar firm, the more notorious Carlyle Group (employer of George H. W. Bush, John Major and James Baker III), began. [6]

Blackstone Chairman Peter G. Peterson is also a Director of the Sony Corporation and a former Director of RCA and General Foods. Interlocking Directorships are how a few interests control many corporations. In 1989 two Reagan Administration officials who were involved in the Iran-Contra scandal, Frank Carlucci and Richard Armitage, became Directors of the Blackstone Group. [7]

Chairman of the Blackstone Group, Chairman of the Council on Foreign Relations, former Chairman of the Federal Reserve Bank of New York

Frank Carlucci is now Chairman of the more well-known Carlyle Group, the 11th-largest contractor with the U.S. Defense Department. The Carlyle Group's promotional hand-outs tout its ' vast, interlocking, global network of businesses and investment professionals. ' On 9/11/01 the Carlyle Group's investors' conference was taking place at the Ritz-Carlton in Washington, DC. *Red Herring* magazine described events there thus: ' As the Carlyle investors watched the World Trade towers go down, the group's prospects went up. ' [8]

The Blackstone Group's Chairman, "Pete" Peterson, now 77, could hardly be more integral to a national and international power-structure. Mr. Peterson's past and present connects to nominally public (U.S. Government Administrations, the Lehman Brothers investment-bank) and overtly secretive organizations (the Council on Foreign Relations, the Bilderberg Group) central to workings of the Western material world. Until 2004 Peter G. Peterson was also Chairman of the Federal Reserve Bank of New York, the most consequential of the 12 regional banks of the Federal Reserve System.

To understand how we in the United States have been put in a fix that makes crimes such as the attacks of 9/11/01 inevitable, we must understand the Federal Reserve System and the Federal Reserve Bank of New York. In The Secrets of the Federal Reserve (a book so revealing that all 10,000 copies of its first German edition were burned in 1955 with the approval of the U.S. High Commissioner to Germany, James B. Conant), U.S. Air Force veteran Eustace Mullins wrote that ' Because the Federal Reserve Bank of New York sets interest rates and controls the daily supply and price of currency throughout the U.S., the owners of that bank are the real directors of the entire system. ' [9]

The Federal Reserve System, the United States' third version of a privatized, central bank, came into being through an Act of Congress on December 22, 1913. This Act's main legislative sponsor was Senator Nelson Aldrich of Rhode Island, son-in-law of the United States' first billionaire, John D. Rockefeller, and uncle of David and Nelson Rockefeller. Despite its name, the "Fed" and its banks are not part of the U.S. Government. Nor is the System publicly owned. Nor has it ever been taxed or audited. At the time of the passage of the Act that created the F.R.S. Congressperson Charles A. Lindbergh Sr. stated: ' " The worst legislative crime of the ages is perpetrated by this banking and currency bill. " ' [10] Lindbergh's condemnation echoed that of 19th-century U.S. leaders toward the first and second versions of a private, central bank for the nation.

> Our whole banking system I ever abhorred, I continue to Abhor, and I shall die abhorring.... Every bank of discount, every bank by which interest is to be paid or profit of any kind made by the [lender], is downright corruption. It is taxation for the public for the benefit and profit of individuals.

> John Adams in 1811, successfully opposing renewal of the charter for a central bank of the United States [11]

> Andrew Jackson will never recharter that monster of corruption! Sooner than live in a country where such a power prevails, I would seek asylum in the wilds of Arabia.

> Andrew Jackson in 1834, refusing to recharter the Second Bank of the United States. [12]

Who and what, then, own the "Fed"? For whom and for what did "Pete" Peterson of the Blackstone Group work?

According to Eustace Mullins and to the U.S. House of Representatives Banking Committee Staff Report of August 12, 1976, ownership of the Federal Reserve Board's 12 regional banks belongs mostly to several private banks or investment banks that are themselves controlled by a relatively few families. More than 25% of the first 203,053 shares in the Federal Reserve Bank of New York, issued on May 19, 1914, were taken by banks controlled by the Morgan and Rockefeller (and thus the Rothschild) families—the Chase Bank and the National City Bank and the First National Bank. [13] In 1955 the latter two banks merged into what's now Citigroup. In 1997 Eric Samuelson recorded that the Chase Manhattan Bank owned 32.35% and that Citibank owned 20.51% of the Federal Rerseve Bank of New York's 19,752,655 shares. That is, majority ownership of the "Fed" still rested with institutions controlled by the Rockefeller and Morgan families. [14]

FEDERAL-RESERVE.NET

Eustace Mullins' book, more that forty years of
work, is available online at www.federal-reserve.net.

In his invaluable Secrets of the Federal Reserve Mullins wrote: ' The shareholders of these banks which own the stock of the Federal Reserve Bank of New York are the people who have controlled our political and economic destinies since 1914. They are the Rothschilds, Lazard Freres (Eugene Mayer), Israel Sieff, Kuhn Loeb Company, Warburg Company, Lehman Brothers, Goldman Sachs, the Rockefeller family, and the J.P. Morgan interests. ' [15] Foremost among them is the family who funded the formation of both the above-named investment and/or commercial banks and the industrial corporations (Standard Oil, U.S. Steel, General Electric, many Railroads, ...) through which the fortunes of famous families such as the Rockefellers, Morgans, Stanleys, Hearsts and Bushes were amassed from the 19th century onward. This family is the Rothschilds—formerly the Bauers—who made their early fortunes from financing wars in the late 18th and early 19th centuries and who then gained control of European central banks.

A book that
further exposes
the Federal
Reserve
System

Book, DVD/VHS
on global money
manipulation

The Federal Reserve System is funded by U.S. taxpayers. Each year the F.R.S. receives more than $250 billion in individuals' taxes to the Internal Revenue System. The "Fed" has also the exclusive license to print U.S. currency—a license that also brought its owning banks and controlling families enormous profits within the span of two World Wars and one global Depression. In 1949 Eustace Mullins wrote that ' the increase in the assets of the Federal Reserve Banks from 143 million dollars in 1913 to 45 billion dollars in 1949 went directly to the private stockholders of the banks '. [16] In 2002, referring to the Federal Rsserve Board and its private banks, Henry Makow wrote: ' Last year alone, the American people paid $360 billion in interest to the bankers. ' [17]

What does the "Fed" do in return for reaping such revenue? It prints money at a cost to itself of $20.62 per one thousand bills of any denomination. That is, the "Fed" may choose to print 1000 $10,000-bills and thereby possess $1 billion at a cost to itself of $20.62. It may then make that $1 billion into $7.7 billion through the device of "fractional banking", a device that lets central banks claim and loan 7.7 times more than an amount of capital they possess. The "Fed" may then further increase its profits by loaning this $7.7 billion to other private banks and to the U.S. Government at interest rates which it itself sets.

You may now see why financier Nathaniel Mayer Rothschild said after he'd gained control of the Bank of England in the early 19th century: ' " I care not what puppet is placed upon the throne of England ... The man who controls the British money supply controls the British Empire, and I control the British money supply. " ' [18] You may see why James Madison warned: ' " History records that the money-changers have used every form of abuse, intrigue, deceit, and violent means possible to maintain their control over governments by controlling money and its issuance. " ' [19]

Mayer Amschel Rothschild, founder of Rothschild financial empire

You may see why Abraham Lincoln and John F. Kennedy briefly returned control of the printing of U.S. currency to the U.S. Government. You may now see more reason why these two Presidents were assassinated.

> Government, possessing power to create and issue currency.... need not and should not borrow capital at interest.... The privilege of creating and issuing money is not only the supreme prerogative of the government but it is the government's greatest creative opportunity.

Abraham Lincoln in 1862 on his Administration's issuance of $450 milllion in interest-free "greenbacks". [20]

Such is the nature—the secretive, usurious, destructive nature—of one business where one beneficiary of " '9/11' ", Peter G. Peterson, Chairman of the Blackstone Group and of the Federal Reserve Bank of New York, works.

Peter G. Peterson was a sumna cum laude graduate of Northwestern University in 1947, Vice-President of the McCann-Erickson advertising agency at age 27, and President of the Bell and Howell electronics research and manufacturing Corporation at age 34. He was Secretary of Commerce in the second Nixon Administration between 1972-73. He was then Chairman and Chief Executive Officer of Lehman Brothers between 1973-77 and then Chairman and CEO of the merged Lehman Brothers, Kuhn, Loeb Inc. between 1977-84. [21] Thus, as CEO of two of the Federal Reserve System's principal share-holding banks, he must have known who fed from the "Fed" and how they did so.

"Pete" Peterson—President of the Concord Coalition and founding Chairman of the Institute for International Economics, father of five children and husband of Joan Ganz Cooney, she the 'Chairman' of the Executive Committee of Children's Television Workshop (which produces *Sesame Street* and *Electric Company*) —is also now the Chairman of the Council on Foreign Relations, a body of U.S.-based executives that itself could hardly be more integral to a national and international—that is, a supranational—power structure.

The quarterly published by the Council on Foreign Relations

These five presidents and others: all members of the Council on Foreign Relations

Since its creation in 1921 the Council on Foreign Relations, the CFR, has had more than 100 of its members in the Cabinets of U.S. Administrations. Presidents Roosevelt, Eisenhower, Kennedy, Nixon, Carter, George H. W. Bush, and Clinton have belonged to the CFR. All but one Director of the Central Intelligence Agency has been a CFR member since the CIA's creation in 1947. Derections by the CFR have preceded identical movements by the U.S. Government, including that to enter into World War II, that to enter the Korean War, that to proceed with the Vietnam War, and that to create the "Carter Doctrine" that the U.S. would intervene militarily to protect its flow of oil from the Middle East.

In 1962 journalist Richard Rovere summarized the CFR's power in *Esquire* magazine: ' The directors of the CFR make up a sort of Presidium for that part of the Establishment that guides our destiny as a nation. '

Under the guise of promoting peace and prosperity the CFR has instead promoted wars that have most profited the bankers who are its leading members. An internal memo of the CFR in August 1941 advised: ' Thus, if war aims are stated which seem to be concerned solely with Anglo-American imperialism, they will offer little to the people in the world.... The interests of other peoples should be stressed ... This would have a better propaganda effect. ' [22]

At this time in 1941 CFR members W. Averill Harriman and Prescott Bush (father of George H. W. Bush and grandfather of George W. Bush) were continuing to profit from their Union Banking Corporation's controlling investment in the Silesian American Corporation and its use of Nazi-run slave labor at Auschwitz for mining in Poland. [23]

Four months after the August 1941 CFR memo about disguising ' war aims ... concerned solely with Anglo-American imperialism ' came the Japanese attack on Pearl Harbor, an attack provoked and allowed by CFR member Franklin Delano Roosevelt. This ' "day of infamy" ' and earlier mass murder killed more than 3000 U.S. citizens and served as the 'pretext' for launching the U.S. into World War II. [24]

Senator Prescott Bush with President Dwight D. Eisenhower

Regarding the Roosevelt Adminstration's foreknowledge of the attack on Pearl Harbor, the Army Review Board found in October 1944: ' Now let us turn to the fateful period between November 27 and December 6, 1941. In this period numerous pieces of information came to our State, War, and Navy Departments in all of their top ranks indicating precisely the intentions of the Japanese including the probable exact hour and date of the attack... Everything that the Japanese were planning to do was known to the United States. ' [25]

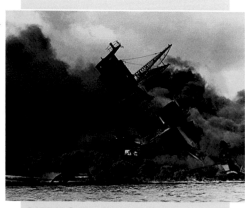

2403 U.S. fatalities resulted from the attack at Pearl Harbor.

According to Charles Higham's <u>Trading With the Enemy</u>, U.S.-based corporations sold crucial materials to Nazi Germany even after the U.S. entered World War II. Standard Oil of New Jersey (Chevron), controlled by Rockefellers, Rothschilds, and the I.G. Farben company of Germany, supplied Nazi Germany with oil. International Telephone and Telegraph (ITT) supplied Nazi Germany with 30,000 to 50,000 fuzes per month for artillery-shells. Ford and General Motors profited from their sudsidiaries' continuing to build tanks for Nazi Germany. [26] And Prescott Bush (after World War II a U.S. Senator from Connecticut) and W. Averill Harriman (after World War II the Governor of New York State before Nelson Rockefeller) continued to profit from Auschwitz slave labor into August of 1942. [27]

In 1950 the *Chicago Tribune* wrote that the members of the Council on Foreign Relations ' have used the prestige that their wealth, their social position, and their education have given them to lead their country toward bankruptcy and military debacle. They should look at their hands. There is blood on them—the dried blood of the last war and the fresh blood of the present one. ' [28]

In 1950, too, David Rockefeller—youngest son of John D. Rockefeller Jr. and grandson of the United States' first billionaire—became Vice-Chairman of the Council on Foreign Relations, a position he held until becoming Chairman of the CFR in 1969. In 1955 (the year in which First National Bank and National City Bank merged toward what's now become Citigroup) [29] David Rockefeller became Vice President in his family's Chase Bank. In 1956 he formed the Lower Manhattan Development Corporation to build a financial nexus in southern Manhattan beside the Chase Bank's new headquarters. He used the New York State power of his brother Nelson (who became Governor in 1958) first to fund construction of the World Trade Center complex through the Port Authority (wiping out a cluster of electronics retailers known as "Radio Row" in the process) and then to occupy the Twin Towers with New York State employees once the Towers were completed (at cost of 62 workers killed) in 1973. [30]

David
Rockefeller

the Twin
Towers under
construction

We know that by 20001 the World Trade Center Buildings needed more than $1 billion in renovations to compete as desirable office space in lower Manhattan. [31]

Let's return now to those parts of the world's economy that have most profited from the attacks of 9/11/01. According to Britain's *The Independent* newspaper on February 29, 2004, the three most profitable commodities traded in the year 2003 were petroleum products, armaments, and illegal narcotics.

Many of us already know that the quarterly earnings of the biggest oil-and-gas corporations surged after the U.S./U.K. invasions of Afghanistan and Iraq. *Business Week* of 2/23/04 reported that 2003 U.S. corporate profits were the largest in 31 years, led by 'Big Oil': ' The group's earnings more than doubled, to $45.2 billion. Exxon Mobil Corp. accounted for the bulk of the industry's gain and ranked No. 1 in total profits: Earnings rose 90%, to $21.5 billion, on a 22% increase in sales, to $222.9 billion. ' We also know that profits by sub-contractors to the largest oil-and-gas

company	2002	2003
Royal Dutch/Shell	4.5	8.2
ExxonMobil	4.7	17.2
British Petroleum	3.4	5.9
Chevron Texaco	1.1	3.5

Net incomre of major oil companies for first six months in billions of dollars. *USA Today*, 8/28/03

corporations, such as Halliburton and Schlumberger, have surged. All these corporations share in the flow of oil and gas from war-torn Iraq. ChevronTexaco showed a record quarterly profit in the first three months of 2004, $2.56 billion, as the price of gas in the U.S. rose despite the output of oil from Iraq also rising toward its pre-invasion level of 2.4 million barrels a day. [32]

In 1972, long before the enormous corporate mergers of the past decade, the then Chase Manhattan Bank held 5.2% of the voting stock of Mobil Oil and 4.5% of Atlantic Richfield (now Arco). Through ownership of shares or membership on Boards of Directors, the Rothschild, Rockefeller, and Morgan families also controlled the largest U.S. insurance, pharmaceutical and food corporations in 1972. [33]

Many of us also know that profits have surged since 9/11/01 for corporations which manufacture weapons. Department of Defense awards for the top five weapons contractors grew from $43.5 billion in 2001 to $66.4 billion in 2003. [34] During the first 24 hours of the 2003 war on Iraq the U.S. fired 500 of Raytheon's Tomahawk missiles at a cost of $600,000 per missile. [35]

company	2001	2002	2003
Locheed Martin	14.7	17.0	21.9
Boeing	13.3	16.6	17.3
Northrop Grumman	5.2	8.7	11.1
General Dynamics	4.7	7.0	8.2
Raytheon	5.6	7.0	7.9
totals	43.5	56.3	66.4

Department of Defense contract awards to top five corporations in billions of dollars.

Much less known by the general public are the profits made from the world's other most traded commodity, illegal narcotics—that is, "Dope."

By far the greatest surge in the trade of illegal narcotics since 2001 —dwarfing even the revenue from coca-derivatives cocaine and Crack—has come from Afghan-grown opium. In fact, the amounts that finally accrue each year from Afghan-grown opium-unto-heroin dwarf the annual global profits from oil-and-gas and armaments.

seed pod of opium poppy

In the Chain of Dope from Afghan farmer to street-corners of the modern industrial world and then to offshore banks, the profits from Afghan-grown opium-unto-heroin have amounted to more than $180 bllion per year since 2002.

This already staggering amount is then enlarged by a "pop" or multiple of 20, we'll see, when profits from opium-unto-heroin are laundered into legal corporations that are traded on Stock Markets.

Before we trace the stages and do the arithmetic by which these profits accrue—and accrue to banks most of all, again—we should briefly review the role of opium in Afghanistan over the past 25 years.

How did opium become so enormous a cash-crop in Afghanistan and this cash-crop then become so important to the world's legal economy? Who helped it become so enormous and important?

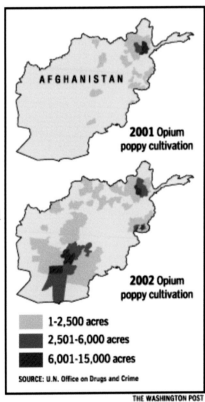

AFGHANISTAN

2001 Opium poppy cultivation

2002 Opium poppy cultivation

1-2,500 acres
2,501-6,000 acres
6,001-15,000 acres

SOURCE: U.N. Office on Drugs and Crime

THE WASHINGTON POST

During the CIA-funded-and-equipped war by Islamic Mujahedeen against forces from the Soviet Union that occupied Afghanistan in the 1980s, Afghanistan became the world's leading territory for cultivation of the poppy plants that produce opium. According to Alfred McCoy, author of an earlier, great exposé, <u>The Politics of Heroin in Southeast Asia</u>, ' The Pakistan-Afghanistan borderlands became the world's top heroin producer, supplying 60 per cent of U.S. demand.... CIA assets again controlled this heroin trade. As the Mujahedeen guerrillas seized territory inside Afghanistan, they ordered peasants to plant opium as a revolutionary tax. Across the border in Pakistan, Afghan leaders and local syndicates under the protection of Pakistan Intelligence operated hundreds of heroin laboratories. During this decade of wide-open drug dealing, the U.S. Drug Enforcement Agency in Islamabad failed to instigate major seizures or arrests. ' [36]

Heroin is a semi-synthetic compound produced from morphine. Unlike morphine heroin can be smoked and injected. The unpredictable potency and purity of illicit heroin results in thousands of deaths per year.

Often present in Islamabad during these years was a former Navy SEAL, Richard Armitage, whom the secretary of drug-lord Khun Sa named as the U.S. overseer of the opium trade from the Golden Crescent of Southeast Asia during the 1970s. [37] Richard Armitage, reported to be a CIA asset since the 1970s, is now Deputy Secretary of State to his friend from Vietnam, Colin Powell.

In 1994 the Muhjadeen warlords who then controlled Afghanistan reaped profits from an annual production of 3400 metric tons of opium raised on 71,470 hectares of poppy fields. (1 hectare = 2.471 acres.) The crop's value to its growers and their lords in 1994 was about $1 billion, based on a price of $350 per kilogram. Its value was much greater to wholesalers and retailers of heroin and to banks and other corporations and to Stock Markets farther along the Chain of Dope.

Richard Armitage beside Colin Powell

How much profit was being made? In 1994 the global trade in illegal narcotics ' was of the same order of magnitude as the global trade in oil ', according to Michel Chossudovsky in Global Outlook, April 2004. In 1998 the United Nations' Drug Control Program estimated that 'the worldwide annual turnover of narcotics' was worth $400 to $500 billion. [38]

In the year 2000 the flow of revenue from Afghan-grown opium was cut drastically. Afghanistan's Taliban government—made up of strict Muslims who had driven out the warlords three to four years earlier—prohibited opium-growing within their territory. The eradication was such a sweeping success that on October 12, 2001 the United Nations Office of Drug Control reported to the General Assembly: ' We now have the results of our annual ground survey of poppy cultivation in Afghanistan. This year's production [2001] is around 185 tons. This is down from the 3300 tons last year [2000], a decrease of over 94 per cent. Compared to the record harvest of 4700 tons two years ago, the decrease is well over 97 per cent. '

October 12, 2001 was five days after the U.S. and Great Britain began to bomb Afghanistan in supposed retaliation for the Taliban's supposed involvement in al Quada's supposed perpetration of " '9/11' ".

By November of 2001 U.S.-supported warlords of ' "the Northern Alliance' " again controlled Afghanistan's prime land for poppy fields. On 11/25/01 the U.K.'s *Observer* newspaper ran this headline: ' Victorious Warlords Set To Open the Opium Floodgates. ' The *Observer* wrote that the warlords were encouraging farmers to plant ' as much opium as possible '. The chart on the right shows what happened. Annual production of Afghan opium grew by about 2000% between 2001 and 2002. In 2003 Afghanistan was back to 3400 metric tons grown per year. According to the U.N. Office of Drug Control, these 3400 metric tons generated ' an income of one billion US dollars for farmers and US $1.3 billion for traffickers '. [39]

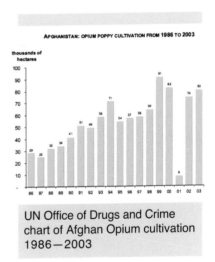

UN Office of Drugs and Crime chart of Afghan Opium cultivation 1986—2003

Profits were times greater farther along the Chain of Dope. According to the U.S. State Department, as quoted by Voice of America on February 27, 2004, " Afghan heroin sells on the international narcotics market for 100 times the price farmers get for their opium right out of the field. " [40]

The money from such sales then goes into the world's major banks. ' The multi-billion dollar revenue of narcotics are deposited in the Western banking system, ' Michel Chossudovsky states. ' Drug money is laundered in the numerous offshore banking havens in Switzerland, Luxembourg, the British Channel Islands, the Cayman Islands and some 50 other locations around the globe. It is here that the criminal syndicates involved in the drug trade and the representatives of the world's largest commercial banks interact.... ' [41]

As one instance, Raul Salinas Gortari, brother of Mexico's then-president, Carlos Salinas Gortari, laundered $87 million through his CitiBank accounts between 1992 and 1994. [42]

Raul Salinas Gortari with friend aboard boat

We come now to the last great multiple in the Chain of Dope—the multiple of "pop". According to Catherine Austin Fitts, a former member of the Board of Directors at the Dillon, Read investment-banking firm and a former Assistant Secretary of the U.S. Department of Housing and Urban Development in the George Herbert Walker Bush Administration (1989-90) : ' The power of narco dollars comes when you combine drug trafficking with the stock market. '

Ms. Fitts breaks down how "pop" works: ' The "pop" is a word I learned on Wall Street to describe the multiple of income at which a stock trades. So if a stock like PepsiCo trades at 20 times its income, that means for every $100,000 of income it makes, its stock goes up $2 million.... On Wall Street, it's all about "pop".... So if I have a company that has a $100,000 of income and a stock trading at 20 times earnings, if I can find a way to run $100,000 of narcotics sales by a few teen-agers in West Philadelphia through my financial statements, I can get my stock market value to go up from $2 million to $4 million. I can double my "pop". ' [43]

We can now see how and why opium production in Afghanistan—and heroin addiction in West Philadelphia—might matter to bankers such as Peter G. Peterson and David Rockefeller. We can now more see why bankers might welcome the 'pretext' for an invasion of Afghanistan as the New York Stock Exchange and NASDAQ plummeted in August 2001. We can also see why in June of 1999 the President of the New York Stock Exchange, Richard Grasso, flew more than 2000 miles to meet with Colombia's largest guerrilla organization, the FARC.

NYSE President Richard Grasso and FARC Chief Raul Reyes embracing

The FARC was then supposed to be taxing the multi-million-dollar trade in coca by Colombian growers. Richard Grasso told the Associated Press that he brought the FARC ' " a message of cooperation from U.S. financial services " '. [44] The FARC, however, rejected Grasso's overture, arguing that decriminalization of coca and cocaine offered a more humane and rational solution.

Now that we can see how financiers' needs involve Stock Markets with criminal traffic in heroin and cocaine, let's look at the fourth and most exploitative support of their G. O. D. D. structure—debt.

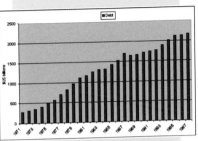

Graph of developing nations's external debt, 1971-1997.
'Vital Signs 1999', Worldwatch Institute

Let's first look outside the U.S. Using the International Monetary Fund and the World Bank as their instruments, the major private banks of the West have been sustained since the late 1970s by extortionate payments on loans to nations of the " 'Third World' " and " 'South' ". In October of 1979 the I.M.F.'s new head, Paul Volcker (member of the Council on Foreign Relations, the Trilateral Commission, and the Bilderberg Group) raised interest rates on loans to developing nations such as Argentina, Brasil and Mexico. Volcker's move combined with the second " 'shock' " of oil-price rises to cause the " 'Third World Debt Crisis' " in the 1980s. Volker was David Rockefeller's choice to head the I.M.F. The I.M.F. then imposed S.A.P.s (Structural Adjustment Programs) on debtor-nations. These S.A.P.s required privatization of nations'industries, surrender of nations' natural resources, and cuts to their funding of programs for education, sanitation and health-care. In return nations received more loans and debt. Thus the S.A.P.s deprived more millions of people of food and water.

The I.M.F. and all major creditor-banks (Bank of America, Chase Manhattan, etc.) also required that payments be in U.S. dollars. Between 1980 and 1986, 109 debtor-nations paid $326 billion in interest and $322 billion in principal, a total of $658 billion, on loans of $430 billion. And yet—due to interest compounding at rates that might shame a loan-shark—they still owed $882 billion by end of 1986. The 1990s worsened conditions. Argentina's foreign debt was $62 billion in 1990 and $146 billion in 2000. Brasil's foreign debt went from $120 billion to $240 billion during the same decade—at the same time as these and many other nations were paying each year amounts about three times more than the amount of the financial aid that they received. [45]

While such usurious cruelty went on internationally, U.S. taxpayers were losing staggering amounts within their government. Both the Clinton and George W. Bush Administrations oversaw huge losses from government offices—a total estimated by Michael C. Ruppert of *From the Wilderness Publications* publications to be $4.1 trillion between 1999-2002—$1.1 trillion from the Department of Defense in 1999, $59 billion from the Departrment of Housing and Urban Development in 1999, $34 billion from Social Security in 2001, $160 billion from Social Security in 2002, ... $845 billion will be taken from Social Security in the year 2010, the *Washington Post* estimates. [46]

And yet—despite the billions unto trillions of dollars taken from ordinary people outside and inside the United States—this nation's government and its major banks themselves carry enormously mounting debt. In 2002 the U.S. Government ran a deficit of more than $480 billion—against a surplus of $3 billion in 1996. In 2002 the U.S. trade deficit was $480 billion—against a $2 billion surplus in 1970. The U.S. debt now stands at $5.9 trillion—up from $0.9 trillion in 1980. Debt of state and local governments and individual consumers in the U.S. is similarly colossal. [47]

Citigroup, the Bank of America, and JP Morgan Chase (the Morgan and Rockefeller families' key banks merged on the last day of 2000), are each at risk in liabilities for many times more than their worth in assets. Around the year 2000, as global oversupply in industries (cars, clothes, computers...) and the " 'Dot-Com Bust' " coincided, each Bank bolstered its bottom line by earning fees for assuming financial responsibility for other companies' risks. They assumed 'derivatives'. As of July 2002 Citigroup held $1 trillion (1000 billion) in assets and $9 trillion at risk. Bank of America then held $620 billion in assets and $10 trillion at risk. JP Morgan Chase held $799 billion in assets and $23.5 trillion at risk. JP Morgan Chase's amount at risk was thus four times the total debt of the U.S. Government! On a single day, July 23, 2002, JP Morgan Chase lost 18.1% of its value in trading on the New York Stock Exchange. [48]

Since July 2002, the U.S./U.K. have invaded Iraq and gained control of Iraqi oil, and two Afghan opium harvests have arrived with their "pop". Most crucial for the U.S. economy, however, have been massive infusions of currency and credit from the Federal Reserve System. Recent infusions portend a crisis more severe than the Crash of 1929. After the business week of May 28, 2004, analyst Robert McHugh of Mainline Investments wrote: ' *the Federal Reserve has confirmed our Stock Market Crash forecast by rasing the Money Supply (M3) by crisis proportions, up another $46.8 billion this past week.... This is unprecedented, unheard-of pre-catastrophe expansion. M-3 is up an amount that we've never seen before without a crisis—$155 billion over the past 4 weeks, a 22.2 annualized rate of growth!!!* ' McHugh continued: ' There was only one other time we saw this level of M-3 growth over a six week period in the history of the United States and that was *AFTER 9/11/01.* ' [49]

Outstanding consumer and financial sector debt between 1980 and 2003.

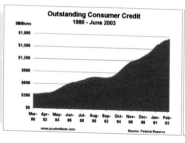

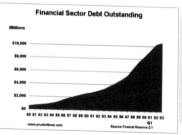

Wars in old times were made to get slaves. The modern implement of imposing slavery is debt.

Ezra Pound [50]

Forgive us our debts, as we forgive our debtors.

Mahalia Jackson sings the 'Lord's Prayer' in "Jazz on a Summer's Day" [51]

We should here remember five sets of facts.

One set is that the Crash of 1929 was itself engineered by the Federal Reserve System through its extending massive amounts of currency and credit to the U.S. public from 1923 onward (" 'the Roaring 20s' ") and then contracting the money-supply sharply in September 1929. Member banks of the "Fed" then refused the public loans at the same time as they demanded payment of debts. The " 'Depression' " ensued, costing 25% of the public their jobs and hundreds of thousands their homes and/or farms. [52] The head of the "Fed" in the 1920s was Paul Warburg, one crafter of the Act that created the Federal Reserve System in 1913. We should also remember that in the 1920s, Paul Warburg's brother Max headed the central bank of Germany, the other nation most impacted by economic collapse circa 1929, and that Max Warburg was a leading partner of Republican Prescott Bush's and Democrat W. Averill Harriman's in Nazi Germany. [53] After World War II Paul Warburg's son, James Paul Warburg, another banker and CFR member, helped to fund mind-control programs through the Tavistock Institute. In 1950, James Paul Warburg told the U.S. Senate Foreign Relations Committee: " We shall have world government, whether we like it or not. " [54]

A second set of facts are the past few years' warnings and preparations toward ' "another terrorist attack" '. Warren Buffet—shown with Lord Jacob Rothschild and Arnold Schwarzengger on page 33—warned in April 2002 that a nuclear attack by " 'al Quada' " inside the U.S. was ' "inevitable" '. [55] Vice-President Dick Cheney told the World Affairs Council in Los Angeles on January 15, 2004 that the next 'terrorist attack' might cost ' " tens of thousands or even hundreds of thousands of lives " '. [56] On that same day, January 15, 2004, the New York Post reported that Homeland Security Secretary Tom Ridge had dined in Manhattan with the heads of ABC, CBS, CNN and Fox News' departments and Network anchors Aaron Brown, Tom Brokaw, and Peter Jennings at Steven Brill's home ' to discuss how they'll cover the next terrorist attack '.

A third set of facts are the proofs in this short book and elsewhere that the Twin Towers and WTC 7 were demolished by internal explosives; that thousands of people in those Buildings were thus murdered; and that " 'al Quada' " could not have executed these demolitions and mass murders.

A fourth set of facts concerns our human species' devastation of planet Earth. Our Oceans are dying. Our Poles are melting. Our ozone is ever more rent. In July 2002 the *Observer* newspaper of Britain wrote that a study by the World Wildlife Fund " warns that the human race is plundering the planet at a pace that outstrips its capacity to support life.... The report, based on scientific data from across the world, reveals that more than a third of the natural world has been destroyed by humans over the past three decades. " [57] Climate models by the U.S. Department of Energy predict that temperatures worldwide will rise 6 degrees Fahrenheit by the year 2050—a rise sure to cause unprecedented disasters and extinctions. [58]

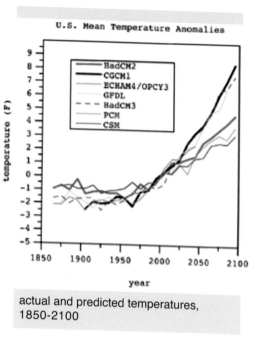

actual and predicted temperatures, 1850-2100

A fifth set of facts are the evident shortfalls in supplies of oil and natural gas that look likely to further pressure international relations and produce catastrophes for ordinary people in the next decade. [59]

What all these sets of facts add up to is: we need to change our ways.

The great news remains that we can still determine our own futures.

Consumption of corporate goods by we who are relatively well-off sustains the system of Systems that's robbing and killing us. Financiers' essentially bankrupt system of Systems has nowhere to go in the future but from one crisis to the next, one war to the next. We'll suffer one more " '9/11' " —in Bali, in Madrid, ...—after another in order to keep us deluded, afraid and obedient.

We need, however, to wake up NOW. Now that we know the true horrors of what happened in New York City on 9/11/01 we need to wake up from the traumas and deceits that have been imposed on us over the past 40 or more years. We need to reject the insanity and impossibility of a 'New World Order' ruled by bankers and their life-denying systems. We need to turn to alternatives that are already working.

Cooperative Solutions

" There is no ' I am. '
There is only ' We are. ' "
—Mumia Abu Jamal, one
of many political prisoners
in the U.S., in Lee Lew
Lee's documentary *All
Power to the People*

" We are valuable... Every
one of us are responsible,
whether we want to be or
whether we don't want to
be ... " —Jeannette
Armstrong, on the casette
compilation *Your Silence
Will Not Protect You*

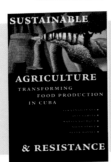

' To understand Cuban agricultural development we must first
look at the richness of detail in this volume. Then we have to
step back and squint to capture the truly novel pathway of
development that Cuba is pioneering. And then once again we
have to focus in on the details, and glimpse the processes
through which Cuba is creating something truly new and
hopeful for all of humanity. ' —Richard Levins, Professor,
Harvard University School of Public Health [1]

Ithaca Hour currency: eighth hour note. The
Ithaca Hours are among hundreds of local
currencies now at work in the world.

Communities in every hemisphere are succeeding with alternatives to fossil-fuel energy and debt-based finances. They're providing their own power, growing their own food, and using their own means of exchange. They're finding ways out of the global financiers' death-grip.

More than 1900 communities around the world are issuing their own currencies.

The best-known of these currencies within the U.S. are the Ithaca HOURS that are exchanged within a 50-mile radius of Ithaca, New York. More than 50,000 Ithaca HOURS have changed hands since 1991. In Minneapolis, Minnesota another local currency, Community HeroCards, have been used since 1998. Following the 1999 TV broadcast in Japan of a documentary about the Swiss writer Michael Ende, "Ende's Last Message", more than 100 Japanese communities have begun to exchange their own forms of debt-free money. More than 500,000 Earthday bills have changed hands in Tokyo's Shibuya District alone.

Even more direct means of exchange are flourishing—*Barter News* estimated the trade in barter in 1997 to be $650 billion. With the advance of the Internet more possibilities are opening up. By 1995 130 sites in the United Kingdom were engaging in trade without use of commercial banks' money. Check out www.transaction.net/money/community and www.ecomoney.net and www.kaikaku21.com/ohmi/.

Entire nation-states have rejected subjugation to oil-and-gas, corporate drugs and interest-bearing debt.

Cuba turned to organic farming after it lost trade relations with Soviet bloc partners after 1989. ' What is happening in Cuba is the largest conversion in world history from conventional agriculture to organic or semi-organic farming, ' wrote Peter Rosset of Food First, By the year 2000 the city of Havana had 8000 communal gardens cultivated by 30,000 people and Cuba as a whole was producing 93,000 tons of compost per year and feeding itself. According to *The New Farm*: ' No chemicals are used in 68% of Cuban corn, 96% of cassava, 72% of coffee, and 40% of bananas. Between 1998 and 2001,

BBC News reported that tens of thousands marched in Caracas on June 7, 2004 to support Hugo Chavez's populist reforms.

chemicals were reduced by 60% in potatoes, 89% in tomatoes, 28% in onions, and 43% in tobacco. ' [2] Check out BBC News (http://news.bbc.co.uk/1/hi/business1409898.stm) and http://webhost.bridgew.edu/jhayeboh for further reports.

In Venezuela the passage by referendum of a new Constitution in 1999 has
inspired a growth of cooperatives from 1900 in 2001 to 10,000 in July 2003.
There land is being redistributed, womens's development banks are being funded,
and soldiers are building tens of thousands of houses and aiding in Mega Markets
of food at discount prices. In April 2004 Venezuela banned transgenic crops from
its territory, stopping a 500,000-acre project by the Monsanto Corporation.
Nearby in Latin America, indigenous farmers in Bolivia. Peru and Ecuador have
successfully fought the Bechtel and ChevronTexaco corporations respectively in
the 21st century. There's also the example of Zapatista resistance and democracy
in Chiapas, evident to the world since 1994.

Movements for renewable energy are also growing. By
1995 19 German cities with a total population of 5 million
were offering rate-based incentives to promote installation
of photovoltaic cells—that is, solar power. [3] Cooperative,
non-governmental eco-banks in Germany (funded with
more than $100 million from members), Belgium,
Denmark, Spain, and Sweden are creating public-power
free of fossil fuels. [4] In Denmark agricultural
cooperatives and individual farmers have combined under
state direction since 1981 to produce 1000 megawatts of
wind-power annually—while California's wind-powered
generation of electricity has stagnated since 1986 due to
withdrawal of funding and incentives. [5] The Global
Windpower Conference in Chicago in March 2004 found
that: ' Wind power has expanded at an average of 28%
annually over the past five years. The United States added
1,687 megawatts (MW) of clean, renewable wind energy
capacity; Europe added 5,467 MW during the same time
period. ' The European Wind Energy Association predicts:
' a cost reduction in wind electricity from 3.79 e cents/kWh
to a level of 3.03 e cents/kWh by 2010. By 2020, the figure
will have fallen to 2.45 e cents. ' [6] This compares with the
U.S. national average price of electricity of 7.56 cents per
kilowatt-hour in April 2004. [7]

U.S installed windpower
capacity (megawatts)
1981-2003. U.S.
windpower more than
doubled between 2000 and
2003, while even greater
increases in Europe
accounted for 60% of global
growth in 2003.

Mass farming of hemp is being revived on every continent. Substitution of hemp's fiber for wood and paper and metal and plastics could save the forests that let our Earth breathe and the air we all breathe. According to RethinkPaper.org: ' Compared to wood, hemp can also be pulped more efficiently and with fewer environmental impacts. When modern pulping processes and technologies are used, up to 80% of unprocessed hemp can be converted to

European hemp farmer

pulp compared with an average of 43% for wood. This fact, along with hemp's high fiber yield, means that up to four acres of forest can be spared for every acre of hemp grown annually. ' [8]

For most of U.S. history, hemp figured integrally in the nation's well-being. " Make the most you can from the Indian hemp seed and sow it everywhere, " U.S. George Washington told his farm-manager in 1794. Industrialists recognized the plant's usefulness. " The car that grows in the field ", Henry Ford called his 1938 hemp-made prototype that burned vegetable-oil and not gas. Its suppression occurred around the same time as corporate monopolists took control of the U.S. money supply. Leading suppressors of hemp in the U.S. were the Hearst, Mellon, and DuPont families, all of whom had financial stakes in forests, chemicals, and banking that were harmed hemp's popularity. [9] Circumstances of the present day — such as produced the crimes of 9/11/01 — call for the use of every possible healthful resource.

Henry Ford swings an axe at his 1941 car to demonstrate the toughness of a trunk door made of soybean and hemp.

' During World War II, imports of hemp and other materials crucial for producing marine cordage, parachutes, and other military necessities became scarce. In response the U.S. Department of Agriculture launched its "Hemp for Victory" program ... By 1943 American farmers registered in the program harvested 375,000 acres of hemp. ' [10]

As for corporate-controlled media, we can also avoid its contradictions and lies. Local radio, local video, local production of music now have the means to reach around the world. Check out www.webradio.com

As for servitudes imposed by the false " 'free market' " worldwide, billions of working people on every continent are recognizing their losses under neo-colonial " 'globalization' " and resisting financiers' frauds. Check out www.uslaw.com .

In short, a great deal is happening around the world toward rational use of resources and a future that may let our species outlast cockroaches. We can still decide our own futures. First, however, we in all of the world must throw off the tyranny of financiers that's at least two centuries long upon us. What's needed still is more will, more resistance, more independence, more organization from the ground up. More courage. More compassion. More cooperation. More life!

We need to build a mass movement across borders. We need to see that we are the answer, the solution, to the crimes imposed on us. We need to build a mass movement that abandons the systems that are robbing and killing us.

Let " '9/11' "—the crime that was designed to set up another terrible century of exploitation and mass murder under the illusions of race, nation and religion—another century under financiers' systems of Guns, Oil, Drugs and Debt—be the last atrocity our capacities for goodness and genius have to suffer.

' In the center of all, and object of all, stands the Human Being, toward whose heroic and spiritual evolution poems and everything directly or indirectly tend, One World or New. ' [12] —Walt Whitman, American poet

" Consumer power " [13] —Aung San Suu Kyi, Burmese resistance leader

Endnotes

one basic fraud among many

1. For the November 9, 2001 video of Osama the Stout, see: http://www.cnn.com/2001/US/12/13/ret.bin.laden.videotape/ and http://www.npr.org/news/specials/response/investigation/011213.binladen.tape.html . For comparison, see the September 2001 video at http://www.cnn.com/2001/US/09/12/binladen.profile/ and http://news.bbc.co.uk/1/hi/world/south_asia/1585636.stm ; and see the December 1998 interview at http://www.time.com/time/asia/asia/magazine/1999/990111/osama1.html .

Introduction

1. 'Trauma Healing', Eric Brahm, *BeyondIntractability.org*, http://www.beyondintractability.org/m/trauma_healing.jsp .
2. ' "A New Pearl Harbor" ', http://www.ifamericansknew.org/us_ints/nc-pilger.html .
3. 'The Economic Rape of America - Chapter Three', http://adlusa.com/economic_rape_of_america.htm .

WTC 7

1. Hear Rudolph Giuliani at http://www.wireonfire.com/donpaul/ .
2. 'Images of the World Trade Center Site Show Thermal Hot Spots on September 16 and 23, 2001', U.S. Geological Survey, Open File Report OF-01-405, http://pubs.usgs.gov/of/2001/ofr-01-0405/ofr-01-0405.html .
3. 'Interstate Bank Building Fire Los Angeles, California (May 4, 1988)', http://www.iklimnet.com/hotelfires/interstatebank.html
4. 'HEARING CHARTER, Learning from 9/11: Understanding the Collapse of the World Trade Center', House Science Committee, March 6, 2002, http://www.house.gov/science/hearings/full02/mar06/charter.htm .
5. See video "Cover-up in Oklahoma City", Jerry Longspagh, 1998.
6. 'Case Study Relating Blast Effects to the Events of April 19, 1995, Oklahoma City, Oklahoma', quoted in 'Multiple Blasts: More Evidence', William F. Jasper, http://www.all-natural.com/oklahoma.html .
7. 'Burning Questions...Need Answers', *FireEngineering.com*, January 4, 2002, http://911research.wtc7.net/cache/wtc/groundzero/fireengineering_manning.html .
8. 'Rebuilding Begins for 7 WTC Despite Unanswered Questions', Peter Grant, *Wall Street Journal*, July 10, 2002, http://homes.wsj.com/columnists_com/bricks/20020710-bricks.html .
9. 'No Fraud, but Huge Profits Seen in World Trade Center Attacks', Joe Shea, *The American Reporter*, August 1, 2004, reprinting piece from September 2001, http://www.american-reporter.com/2,421W/1494.html .
10. See articles from *Bloomberg News*, *New York Law Journal*, *The American Lawyer*, *Insurance Journal*, and *Newsday* at 'The World Trade Center Towers Collapse as an Enormous Insurnace Scam', http://911review.com/motive/docs/insurance_scam.html .

18 11. See 'Troubling Questions in Troubling Times' by James S. Adam, October 5, 2001, at http://www.serendipity.li/wot/adam.htm for articles from *New York Newsday* and *The New York Times* of 1993 about cassette-tapes made by FBI informant and evident bomb-builder Emad Salem. Attorney Ron Kuby is quoted: " The article on the FBI being involved in the World Trade Center bombing [*New York Times*, 10/28/93] actually understated the evidence, believe it or not. The informer, Emad Salem, is actually on tape saying that he built the bomb that ultimately blew up the World Trade Center....The mastermind is the government of the United States. It was a phony, government-engineered conspiracy to begin with. It would never have amounted to anything had the government not planned it. " Also bearing on 9/11/01: Richard Ben-Veniste, member of the National Commission on Terrorist Attacks, was quoted in the *Washington Post* of October 29, 1993 as saying that the recordings by Emad Salem posed "an absolute nightmare for federal prosecutors". Curiously, however, Emad Salem and his vital bomb-building role is omitted from the three pages that The 9/11 Commission Report, co-authored by Richard Ben-Veniste, devotes to the 1993 WTC bombing. See http://www.questionsquestions.net/docs04/0526_donpaul.html for further parallels between 2/26/93 and 9/11/01. See also 'The Shadow', October 1994, for a piece by Paul DiRienzo, Frank Morales, and Chris Flash.

19 12. "America Rebuilds", http://www.pbs.org/americarebuilds/ .

The Twin Towers

21 1. Cooperative Research timelines, http://www.cooperativeresearch.org/ . Use flight numbers in search tool to view records, eg. 'Flight 175'.

24 2. 'Report: Tape Sheds Light on WTC Rescuers', August 4, 2002, http://www.cnn.com/2002/US/08/04/wtc.firefighters/ .

3. 'We Will Not Forget, A Day of Terror', http://www.chiefengineer.org/article.cfm?seqnum1=1029

4. 'WTC Background Information', *iCivilEngineer*, http://www.icivilengineer.com/News/WTC/background.php .

25 5. 'How the World Trade Center fell', Sheila Barter, *BBC News*, September 13, 2001, http://news.bbc.co.uk/1/hi/world/americas/1540044.stm .

26 6. 'Why Did the World Trade Center Collapse--Simple Analysis', Zdenek P. Bazant and Yong Zhou, commented verstion of article at http://911research.wtc7.net/disinfo/experts/articles/bazant_jem/bazant_zhou.html .

7. 'Fire Resistance of Steel Framed Car Parks', Corus Construction study, *CorusConstruction.com*, http://911research.wtc7.net/cache/wtc/analysis/fires/car_park_tests.htm .

27 8. 'Why Did the World Trade Center Collapse? Science, Engineering, and Speculation', *Journal of the Minerals, Metals and Materials Society*, http://www.tms.org/pubs/journals/JOM/0112/Eagar/Eagar-0112.html .

9. 'The Collapse: An Engineer's Perspective', *NOVA Online*, http://www.pbs.org/wgbh/nova/wtc/collapse.html .

32 10. 'Characterization of the Dust/Smoke Aerosol that Settled East of the World Trade Center (WTC) in Lower Manhattan after the Collapse of the WTC 11 September 2001', Paul J Lioy, et. al., *EHP Online*, http://ehp.niehs.nih.gov/members/2002/110p703-714lioy/lioy-full.html .

35 11. 'Thermodynamic Analysis of the Twin Tower Collapses', Jim Hoffman, http://911research.wtc7.net/papers/dustvolume/volume.html .

36 12. 'Closure from 9/11 Elusive for Many', Rick Hampson and Martha T. Moore, USA Today, September 3, 2003, http://www.usatoday.com/news/nation/2003-09-03-sept-11-son_x.htm .

13. '1000 9/11 victims 'never identified'', September 3, 2003, http://www.news.com.au/common/story_page/0,4057,6949759%255E1702,00.html .

The Financiers Behind " '9/11' "

37 1. Anatole Kaletsky, London Times, September 26, 2002.

2. Excerpt from Jefferson to Gallatin letter at http://famguardian.org/Subjects/MoneyBanking/MoneyBanking.htm .

3. Memoirs, David Rockefeller, Random House, 2002, pp. 410-11.

38 4. United States National Archives transcript for September 11, 1990 Joint Session of Congress, http://www.usembassy.de/usa/etexts/speeches/rhetoric/gbaggres.htm .

5. Council on Foreign Relations, Transcript of September 14, 2001 General Meeting in Washington, D.C., http://tinyurl.com/5hja5 .

39 6. See www.hoovers.com for summaries of the Blackstone Group and the Carlyle Group.

7. 'Turning over the rocks at... THE BLACKSTONE GROUP', Al Martin, from The Conspirators: Secrets of an Iran-Contra Insider, http://www.the-catbird-seat.net/BlackstoneGroup.htm .

8. 'Carlyle's Way/ Making a Mint inside "the Iron Triangle" of Defense, Government and Industry', Dan Briody, Red Herring magazine, January 8, 2002.

40 9. The Secrets of the Federal Reserve, Eustace Mullins, Bankers Research Institute, 1984. p. 33.

10. Representative Charles A. Lindbergh speaking in Congress, 1913, http://www.documentationexpress.com/article7-about-money.html .

11. Rothschild: The Wealth and Power of a Dynasty, Derek Wilson, Charles Scribner's Sons, 1988, p. 32.

12. Old Hickory, Burke Davis, Dial Press, 1977, p. 335.

41 13. Mullins, p. 34.

14. 'Central Banking and the Private Control of Money', Eric Samuelson, Nexus, December 1998 - January 1999, p. 12.

15. Mullins, p. 3.

42 16. Mullins, p. 159.

17. 'Banking Cartel is the Cause of Humanity's Woes', Makow, www.bankindex.com/revealing_news/hm/default1.asp .

18. 'Remarkable Remedy', Jean Carpenter, http://www.sonnet.com/usr/kidogo/remedy5.html#It .

19. 'Presidential Quotations', http://www.themoneymasters.com/presiden.htm .

20. The Creature from Jekyll Island, G. Edward Griffin, American Media, 1994, p. 384.

43 21. 'The Honorable Peter G. Peterson, President, The Concord Coalition', http://www.concordcoalition.org/home/petersonbio.html

44 22. When Corporations Ruled the World, David R. Korten, Kumarian Press, 1995, excerpt at http://www.thirdworldtraveler.com/Korten/BuildEliteConsens_WCRW.html .

23. George H.W. Bush: The Unauthorized Biography, G. Webster Tarpley and Anton Chaiken, 1992.

24. <u>Infamy</u>, John Toland, Bantam Dell, 1982, and <u>Day of Deceit: The Truth about FDR and Pearl Harbor</u>, Robert B. Stinnett, Simon & Schuster, 2001.

25. Army Review Board report October 20, 1944, quoted in <u>Pearl Harbor: Mother of All Conspiracies</u>, Mark Emerson Willey, X Libris 2001, report transcribed by Larry W, Jewell and available at http://www.geocities.com/Pentagon/6315/pearl.html .

26. <u>Trading With the Enemy</u>, Charles Higham, Delacorte Press, 1983, pp. 40-41, 59, 99, 162.

27. " '9/11' "/<u>Facing Our Fascist State</u>, Don Paul, I/R, 2002, pp. 40-41, 83.

28. Editorial, *Chicago Tribune*, December 9, 1950.

29. 'Corporate History' at http://www.citigroup.com/citigroup/corporate/history/citibank.htm .

30. <u>Divided We Stand, A Biography of New York'sWorld Trade Center</u>, Eric Darton, Basic Books, 2000, quoted in " '9/11' "/<u>Facing ...</u>, pp. 41-43.

31. 'A New Garden of Eden', http://www.notbored.org/wtc.html , and 'WTC: Danger of Asbestos Fallout', http://www.immuneweb.org/911/articles/moeller.html .

32. *San Francisco Chronicle*, May 1 and May 9, 2004.

33. <u>Power, Inc.</u>, Morton Mintz and Jerry A. Cohen, The Viking Press, 1976, pp. 297-303.

34. Procurement Statistics, Directorate for Information Operations and Reports, http://www.dior.whs.mil/peidhome/procstat/procstat.htm .

35. *Corporate Research E-Letter*, April 2003, Philip Mattera, http://www.corp-research,org/apr03.htm .

36. 'Drug Fallout: the CIA's 40-year Complicity in the Narcotics Trade', Alfred McCoy, *The Progressive*, August 1, 1997.

37. <u>Called to Serve</u>, Colonel Bo Gritz, Lazarus Publishing, 1991, quoted on pp. 126-27, <u>Alice in Wonderland and the World Trade Center</u>, David Icke, Bridge of Love, 2002.

38. 'The Spoils of War: Afghanistan's Multibillion-dollar Heroin Trade', Michel Chossudovsky, www.globalresearch.ca, April 2004.

39. Ibid.

40. Ibid.

41. Ibid.

42. 'Americas Citibank Censured over Money Laundering' *BBC News*, November 9, 99, http://news.bbc.co.uk/1/hi/world/americas/511951.stm .

43. *NarcoNews Bulletin*, October 31, 2002, http://www.narconews.com/narcodollars2.html .

44. 'Wall Street Goes Jungle', Frank Bajak, Associated Press, *Laredo Morning Times*, June 27, 1999, http://www.lmtonline.com/news/archive/0627/pagea1.pdf .

45. William Engdahl, 'How the IMF Props Up the Bankrupt Dollar System', http://www.serendipity.li/hr/imf_and_dollar_system.htm .

46. 'The Gathering Storm', Michael C. Ruppert, *From the Wilderness Publications*, http://www.fromthewilderness.com/free/ww3/FTW-JULY_2002.pdf .

47. See Global Policy Forum data at http://www.globalpolicy.org/socecon/crisis/index.htm .

48. " '9/11' "/<u>Facing ...</u>, pp. 41-43, pp. 92-96.

49. 'Financial Markets Forecast and Analysis', Robert McHugh, http://www.safehaven.com/article-1597.htm .

50. 'The Federal Reserve Bankers', Chapter Three in a variously titled book by Frederick Mann, http://www.mind-trek.com/reports/eco-rape/ch03.htm .

51. "Jazz on a Summer's Day", Bert Stern, New Yorker Films, 1959.

52. 'What Caused the Great Depression of the 1930's?', http://www.shambhala.org/business/goldocean/causdep.html and 'About the Great Depression', http://www.english.uiuc.edu/maps/depression/about.htm .

53. <u>Rule by Secrecy</u>, Jim Marrs, HarperCollins, 2000, pp. 62-63,70-71.

54. 'Tavistock, The Best Kept Secret in America', http://educate-yourself.org/nwo/nwotavistockbestkeptsecret.shtml .

55. 'Buffet Predicts Nuclear Attack' *Sydney Morning Herald* (Australia), May 7, 2002, at http://www.smh.com.au/articles/2002/05/06/1019441477485.html?oneclick=true .

56. 'Cheney's Grim Vision: Decades of War, Vice President Says Bush Policy Aimed at Long-term World Threat', January 15, 2004, *SFGate*, http://tinyurl.com/ytl6f

57. 'Earth Will Expire by 2050', Mark Townsend and Jason Burke, *The Observer*, July 7, 2002, http://observer.guardian.co.uk/international/story/0,6903,750783,00.html .

58. 'US National Assessment of the Potential Consequences of Climate Variability and Change', http://www.usgcrp.gov/usgcrp/nacc/default.htm .

59. 'What Will Be the Next Target of the Oil Coup?', 'Part II in FTW's Series on the End of the Age of Oil', Dale Allen Pfeiffer, http://www.fromthewilderness.com/free/ww3/01_29_02_what_next.html .

Cooperative Solutions

1. Epilogue to <u>Sustainable Agriculture and Resistance: Transforming Food Production in Cuba</u>, edited by Fernando Funes, Luis Garcia, Martin Bourque, Nilda Perez, and Peter Rosset, Food First Books, 2002. See http://www.newformulation.org/2agriculture.htm .

2. 'Cuba's 5th Conference on Organic Agriculture Features the Fruits of a Decade-long Focus on Organic', *The New Farm*, http://www.newfarm.org/international/features/0703/cubaconf.shtml .

3. <u>Who Owns the Sun?</u>, Daniel Berman and John T. O'Connner, Chelsea Green Press, 1995, pp. 231-33.

4. Ibid, p. 233.

5. Ibid, pp. 226-31.

6. 'Wind Force 12 Study', EWEA, p. 74, http://www.ewea.org/03publications/WindForce12.htm, See www.ewea.org and www.awea.org on the growth of power-generation by wind. See http://store.sundancesolar.com/rearerepecrr.html on renewables altogether.

7. 'Annual Electricity Survey Published by NUS Consulting Shows Slight Drop in National Average Price', *The Power Report*, http://tinyurl.com/6u497 .

8. 'HEMP: The Hardy Paper Crop', http://rethinkpaper.org/content/hemp.cfm .

9. <u>Cannabis</u>, Mathias Broeckers, AT Verlag, 2002, pp. 19, 101.

10. "Busted: America's War on Marijuana", *PBS Frontline*, 2000, http://www.pbs.org/wgbh/pages/frontline/shows/dope/etc/cron.html .

11. See globalhemp.com for a directory of information and resources. See 'Hemp: A New Crop with New Uses for North America' by Ernest Small and David Marcus at http://www.hort.purdue.edu/newcrop/ncnu02/v5-284.html for an excellent summary.

12. 'A Backward Glance', last Preface to <u>Leaves of Grass</u>, 1888, <u>The Viking Portable Walt Whitman</u>, The Viking Press, 1973.

13. 'Massachusetts Takes on Burma', Fred Hiatt, *Washington Post*, January 31, 1999, http://www.burmalibrary.org/reg.burma/archives/199902/msg00071.html .

Recommended Resources (an incomplete list)

The Crimes of 9/11/01

Painful Questions, Eric Hufschmid, Endpoint Software, 2002
Inside Job, Jim Marrs, Origin Press, 2003
Alice in Wonderland and the World Trade Center Disaster, David Icke, Bridge of Love, 2002
The New Pearl Harbor, David Ray Griffin, Olive Branch Press, 2004
The War on Freedom, Nafeez Mossaddeq Ahmed, Tree of Life, 2002

"The Great Conspiracy", second edition, Barrie Zwicker
"Painful Deceptions", second edition, Eric Hufschmid
"Truth and Lies of 9/11", Michael Ruppert
"Mohammad Atta and the Venice Flying Circus", Daniel Hopsicker
"9/11 Perspective", Ken Jenkens

www.globalresearch.ca   www.cooperativeresearch.org   www.plaguepuppy.net
www.fromthewilderness.com   www.questionsquestions.net   www.onlinejournal.com

Foreground to the Crimes of 9/11/01

The Globalization of Poverty and the New World Order, Michel Chossudovsky, Global Outlook, 2003
Day of Deceit, Robert B. Stinnett, Simon & Schuster. 2001
Trading with the Enemy, Charles Higham, Delacorte Press, 1983
Infamy, John Toland, Bantam Dell, 1983
Blowback, Christopher Simpson, Weidenfeld and Nicolson, 1988
Wall Street and the Rise of Hitler, 76 Press, 1976, and America's Secret Establishment: An Introduction to the Order of Skull and Bones, Liberty House Press, 1986, Antony Sutton
The Rule of Racialization, Steve Martinot, Temple Unviersity Press, 2003

"Waco: The Rules of Engagement", William Gavlicki
"Cover-Up in Oklahoma City", Jerry Longspagh

The Financiers Behind " '9/11' "

The Creature from Jekyll Island, G. Edward Griffin, American Media, 1994
Rule by Secrecy, Jim Marrs. Harper-Collins, 2000
The Secrets of the Federal Reserve, Eustace Mullins, Bankers Research Institute, 1983
The Money Masters, Bill Still and Patrick S. J. Carmack, 1995 (book, VHS and PAL)

www.bilderberg.com

Cooperative and Spiritual Solutions

Critical Path, R. Buckminster Fuller, St. Martins Press, 1981
Leaves of Grass, Walt Whitman, 1855, introduction by Malcolm Cowley, Viking Press, 1959
Their Eyes Were Watching God, Zora Neale Hurston, 1937, Perennial Classics, 1998
Who Owns the Sun?, Daniel Berman and John T. O'Conner, Chelsea Green, 1996

"All Power to the People", Lee Lew Lee

www.bolivariancircles.net   www.globalhemp.com   www.webradio.com

Acknowledgments and Clarifications

Thanks and a warm hand-shake to all who have communicated any part of the actuality of the " 'Attack on America' ". None of us among researchers into 9/11/01 could advance without the work of many others before us and with us. Uncovering the crimes of that day and related, prior days is of course a collective effort.

We particularly thank the main organizers of the International Inquiry into 9/11—Carol Broulliet in San Francisco, March of 2004, and Barrie Zwicker and Ian Woods in Toronto, May of this year. We also thank the hundreds of '9/11 Truth' activists who have marched in demonstrations and e-mailed our movement's calls for more honest exposure of the 9/11/01 crimes.

Our Resources page lists some of the aids that have helped this book. We think that each listed book or tape or Website offers substantial information and/or illumination. We know, too, that our incomplete memories have missed important resources that will later leap to mind.

We want to make clear that we don't endorse the whole of certain resources that we recommend. While we believe that a conspiracy has operated for more than two centuries in Europe and the United States to direct masses of people's destinies through terror, war, narcotics-traffic, and control of nations' money-supply—and that this conspiracy relates to secret-societies such as the Illuminati, the Order of Skull and Bones, and the Bilderberg Group—we don't believe that the two centuries-worth of financiers, murderers, and drug-dealers in this conspiracy are other than human or more than the groupings of criminal opportunists such as history shows often before the late 18th century. We believe that they're neither descendants of extraterrestrials nor 'reptilian-human hybrids' (as David Icke writes in his informative <u>Alice in Wonderland</u>.) We believe they're just gangsters inside and behind Banks.

We also believe that the United States of its land- and/or slave-owning Founding Fathers was far from an inclusive or ideal society. We believe that the 'Freedom' advocated by many patriots and monetarists' websites must be freedom for every race, gender and trans-gender and we believe that the hundreds of years' labor by Blacks and other slaves in the United States deserves reparations at the least. We believe that the force and spirit known as God made us all to most flourish when free and we believe that the United States of now—a even richer mix than this nation was in 1789 or 1836 or 1863—with women and people of color holding at least the potential on paper for political power—offers a greater promise of equity for itself and for the world.

Finally, we believe that " 'Left' " and " 'Right' " are largely illusions, promoted by the same 'elite' interests who want the crimes and ramifications of 9/11/01 hidden behind a cartoon of alarm (" '9/11' ") that demonizes a largely foreign faith and largely browner people as the Other and that again presses us into roles of us-versus-them. We do have an enemy that we of the " 'Left' " or " 'Right' " should unite to oppose. That enemy, we believe, is the criminal mind-set responsible for producing unnecessary misery worldwide. That enemy is also our acquiescence to it and our sustenance of it.

We still can change. We still have choices. We can choose to stop our dying for criminals whose ends are—we must see from the rising tides and dying crops around us—the mass murder or mass suicide of our children or grandchildren. We must now see that a relatively few criminals killed us by the thousands in the Twin Towers, as a criminal few killed us in Pearl Harbor. They killed us aboard the *Lusitania* and aboard the *Maine*. They killed us in World Wars and Korea and Vietnam. Now they're killing us—Black, White, Yellow, Brown—Christian, Muslim, Animist, Jew—in Afghanistan and Iraq.

Let us stop now. Let us gain some final clarity. Let us stop our buying and selling and killing and dying for insane criminality. Let us begin or regain the religious concept of living one for all—of developing our individual gifts—for the enrichment of our selves, our families, and our societies as wholes.

We can make a good ending yet. Our acquiescence let " '9/11' " happen and our acquiescence lets the lies of " '9/11' " persist. Our resistance, our choices, however, can change everything.